Single

Bethanne Milton

ISBN 978-1-0980-6169-2 (paperback)
ISBN 978-1-0980-6170-8 (digital)

Christian Faith Publishing, Inc.
832 Park Avenue
Meadville, PA 16335
www.christianfaithpublishing.com

Printed in the United States of America

Introduction

When I was two or three years old, I had two boyfriends at the same time. Honest to goodness, I did. It's not even that I have simply been told that story, I actually remember it.

The desire to be loved by others is something that is born in us from the beginning. So is the desire to be loved above all else by one individual person. This is why you see toddlers, like myself at one time, holding hands and giving each other kisses. Most people would tell you that young children simply imitate the adults in their lives. Perhaps, but I believe children understand love. They understand affection in its most basic forms.

If this desire for love and affection, whether through nature or nurture, is something that we acquire from such an early age, why is it important to remain single? The truth is that many people in Christian circles do not see the value of nor do they put an emphasis on singleness.

There is a point during adolescence in the Christian world where "single" seems to become a dirty word. It's something that no one wants to be and everyone tries to get rid of. It is a title that is swiftly discarded, and its discarding is often sealed with a marriage license. Why? How did we come to this place where our dependence and self-worth hinges not on God but on the reciprocated affection of another human being?

Singleness is a gift.

Singleness is a process.

It is in times of embraced singleness that God can reveal to us the fullness of His love for us: His vast, deep, unending love for us.

Chapter 1
Why Am I Alone?

That is *the* question, isn't it? Why am I alone? Why does no one want me? Why doesn't the right person want me? Is there something wrong with me? Am I not good enough? What am I doing wrong?

I have asked myself all of those questions and more since the time I was in middle school. Maybe you have asked yourself similar questions. Think about the reasons and excuses you've come up with for why you are single or have been single. My guess is that more times than not, you have believed that there is something wrong with you, or something you had to change to make people like you. Those feelings stem from insecurities and a lack of self-worth. Don't misunderstand me when I say that. You may truly love yourself, your personality, your talents, and your physical appearance. Loving the person you are overall doesn't mean that you do not have insecurities or that you find yourself worthy of what you deserve.

Loneliness is a powerful influencer. The enemy uses loneliness as a tactic to make us feel inadequate and insufficient. It slowly draws you into a pit where the deeper you are, the more difficult it is to find your way out. How do you get out of a low place like that? The easy answer is to turn to Christ. He is the shepherd that leaves the ninety-nine sheep in search of the one that is lost. He meets us where we are and works within us to bring us out of the dark places that we get ourselves into.

Even though He is truly all that we need, our flesh craves a more practical approach to getting out of the pit of loneliness. The truth that you need to come to and accept is that *singleness does not equal aloneness.* If you think "alone" whenever you think about being single, you have the wrong idea about what both of those words mean. Being alone means isolation; being alone means separation. If you are truly alone, it means that no one knows who you are or cares about what happens to you. Singleness is independence. Singleness is its own type of freedom. It is an opportunity to experience people and the world on your own and at your own pace. It is also an opportunity to embrace and step into what God is calling you to before having to try to balance His call out with another person.

The fact of the matter is that none of us is ever alone. There are always people who care about you. There are always going to be people for you to fall back on when you need them. If you think or feel like you are alone, reflect on the people who go through your life regularly. I doubt that you won't be able to find someone to watch your back.

The (other) fact of the matter is this: even if you are forsaken by every single person on this earth, Christ never forsakes us. No matter how far we stray from Him, He is always constant. I cannot think of a single time in my life where God's hand has not been over it. Even in times where I may not have felt Him in that instant, I have seen His grace and His protection in the end.

In the spirit of changing the attitude toward singleness, dating, and marriage in the church as a whole, throughout this book I am going to share with you a few lessons I have learned in my years of being…unattached. Here is the first:

Lesson 1: Being Single Is Not a Punishment!

Did God plan it out so that we could all enter into a marriage one day? Obviously. Look at Adam. Adam, initially being the only human to exist, was actually alone. God saw that Adam was alone and said, "It is not good that the man should be alone; I will make a helper fit for him" (Gen. 2:18, ESV). God saw Adam's loneliness and saw that it was fixed by giving him a companion, a wife.

Spiritual truth: Just because Adam married the first woman he saw, it doesn't mean you need to.

Translation: Don't settle for less than you deserve or less than God has planned in order to escape a season of "loneliness."

Marriage is something that we often idolize and idealize. Many young people in the church see marriage as their endgame. "I just need to do X, Y, and Z, get married, and then my life will be complete." Wherever or whenever that attitude came about, we need to end it now! Dating and/or marrying someone are not going to fix your life! That attitude is what leads young Christians to believe that if they are still single by the time they are twenty they must be being punished for something. *Punished!* I actually have to laugh at myself when I think back to times when I felt like God was keeping me single because I had done something wrong.

God is not looking to punish you by keeping you single.

I don't believe God is in the business of punishing us in general. What God *is* in the business of is teaching us. God wants us to continually grow in every aspect of our lives. When we go through a time of hardship, it is not because He wants us to suffer, but because He wants us to grow. He wants us to grow in our thinking, grow in our experience, and grow in our faith and trust in Him. This is the same process with singleness. God uses times of being single as an opportunity to teach valuable lessons about self-worth, boundaries, where compromise is okay and is not okay, and about His perfect timing. The key to hearing God's voice clearly in these times is being content and being willing to listen to what He is trying to speak to you. Don't live with an attitude of what you are lacking, but with an attitude of expectancy of what God is teaching you and of what he has for you in the future.

Another important thing to remember is that life is lived in seasons. Seasons of natural joy, and seasons where we have to choose joy. Seasons where we have an overwhelming sense of purpose and drive, and seasons where we can really sit and take time to breathe in the presence of God.

Some seasons in our lives are filled with countless people who have consistent roles, while others are defined by a faithful few people we can count on. One important season that everyone goes through at some point is that of singleness. Seasons of singleness are often coupled with seasons of loneliness, but they are not mutually exclusive. You could be the most popular and well-liked person, beloved by your boyfriend or girlfriend, and adored by your friends and family, yet still feel completely alone. You could also be single and have just a few people who you can count on in your life and feel more loved and fulfilled than people who have the things you're "missing." The truth is that loneliness is most often a state of mind. It takes conditioning and training to overcome the feelings of loneliness that stem from being single and seeing other people around you in relationships. I've been there more times than I can count.

While there are times in my singleness that loneliness creeps its way back into my heart, overall I have found joy and contentment in this time. Why? Because I have learned to find my worth in Christ. How? The phrase "fake it till you make it" comes to mind. I continually told myself that I was content being single, and I took on an attitude of confidence as a single woman. Eventually, that, coupled with a crazy amount of prayer, became true for me. I believed it would be so, and it was. I spoke that joy over my life, and it came.

I'm not saying I never feel sad or lonely anymore. *Trust me*, I do. It comes in waves. It sneaks up from behind and crashes over me. At times it felt like I was drowning in my aloneness, desperately seeking for someone to rescue me, but rescue never came. Not in the way I was wanting. I didn't need to be rescued from my aloneness because I wasn't alone. I didn't need to be rescued from my singleness because it's not something to be rescued from. What I needed to be rescued from was myself; I needed to be rescued from a mindset. Whenever I feel those waves beginning to creep up on me again, I have a God who reminds me of who I am, who He has created me to be, and all of the things He has in store for me.

Seasons of being single do not have to be seasons of being alone. They can be times of immense joy and exponential growth. You are not alone. You do not need a relationship to fulfill you. You do not need a relationship to do ministry. You are loved beyond measure by someone who willingly sacrificed His life to have a relationship with you. Stop speaking singleness over your life as a deficiency and take it as an opportunity to step into a time of spiritual growth.

Chapter 2
What Is Love?

Isn't it funny how we always think we have a good handle on what love is? And yet, invariably, we meet someone new and what we thought we had experienced as love before seems so silly and insignificant. And then that "love" ends and a new and deeper "love" comes along. It is often a long and painstaking process finding real and true love.

We throw that word around a lot in modern culture. We *love* to shop, or we *love* chocolate. We've diluted that word so much that sometimes when we actually do love something, or someone, we have to try to find different words to describe the deepness of that feeling. On one hand, we say how we love everyone and everything, and on the other we have a screwed up version of what love is. The media has had a vicious hold over the lives of its viewers for decades. It dictates how we view ourselves, how we view the world, and how we view relationships. It cheapens love. Music, television, and movies most often put emphasis on the wrong pieces of relationships. Everything seems to be about physical attraction and falling in love at first sight; meeting the person you end up with in some magical and too-good-to-be-true way. Because of this, you expect that that's what love is, and when you aren't finding that kind love, you begin to believe you are unlovable.

We waste a lot of time and energy feeling like we are not loved when the truth of the matter is that we do not understand what love is. To truly understand what love is, we have to look at *who* love is. God is love (1 John 4:7–21). We see this manifest all through the Bible. God's love is what ties each story in the Bible to the next. His love goes by many names—grace, compassion, sacrifice—yet its consistency and steadfastness are unchanging, even to this day.

Without love, we have nothing, and without God, we do not have love. His love is what set the world into motion and is what gives us hope for the future. In fact, our entire faith is based upon a series of the most loving acts to ever take place.

"In this the love of God was made manifest among us, that God sent his only Son into the world, so that we might live through him" (1 John 4:9, ESV).

God sent His son to Earth to be born, to live among us, and to die, all to make a pathway to lead us to Him. *That* is love. *That* is sacrifice. In order to love people and accept love from people, we need to accept that act of love as something done not for a select few but for all. We need to accept that love as our own.

If God is love, and love comes from God, what does it look like? Often, you will hear passages from 1 Corinthians 13 read at weddings to set a precedent for what love should look like in a marriage. While these things are true, this chapter is also a guide for what love should look like in our everyday lives. We are called to "love one another" (John13:34, ESV) as Christ has loved us. This chapter in Corinthians teaches us what it should look like among friends, colleagues, and between believers and nonbelievers. To love others in this way is to be Christ to them.

1 Corinthians 13:4–10, 13
"Love is patient and kind."

Your interactions with other believers and nonbelievers should be defined as times of patience, of understanding, and of kindness.

"*Love does not envy or boast.*"

Be grateful for what you have and rejoice in others' success, lifting up those successes and accomplishments over your own.

"*It is not arrogant or rude.*"

Be humble and be kind in your love, valuing others above yourself.

"*It does not insist on its own way.*"

Love values the opinions of others and includes compromise.

"*It is not irritable or resentful.*"

Love does not anger easily, nor does it hold on to that anger.

"*It does not rejoice in wrongdoing.*"

If you see someone you love doing something that could do them harm, love would have you intervene.

"*But rejoices with the truth.*"

Love rejoices in what is good and right and true.

"*Love bears all things, believes all things, hopes all things, endures all things.*"

We should come to understand that love is all enduring and all trusting. If it wavers, it is not love. If it cannot trust, it is not love.

"*Love never ends.*"

Love never ends.

"*As for prophecies, they will pass away; as for tongues, they will cease; as for knowledge, it will pass away. For we know in part and we prophecy in part, but when perfect comes, partial will pass away*" (ESV).

Earthly gifts will not last forever. They are for now. Love is not just for now.

"*And now these three remain: faith, hope and love. But the greatest of these is love*" (NIV).

When everything from earth fades away, faith, hope, and love will remain, but love will remain above all else.

Every day when we go out into the world, we need to put on love. Colossians chapter 3 tells us to be compassionate, kind, humble, gentle, patient, and forgiving, "And over all these virtues put on love, which binds them all together in perfect unity" (verse 14, NIV). When we put on love in our everyday lives and in every relationship, it binds together each of those qualities in our hearts so that compassion and kindness and humility flow out of us naturally as a result of that love; so that when we truly love someone, we are naturally gentle, patient, and forgiving toward them. Love is what brings forgiveness and what brings redemption. If Christ's love drove Him to die to cover our sins, why can't we love people in simpler ways with the intent of bringing them into a place of restoration? Christ's love covered up our sins and failures. Our love toward other people can draw them closer to the love that Christ has for them.

"Above all, love each other deeply, because love covers a multitude of sins" (1 Pet. 4:8, NIV).

You must be able to understand these types of love, exercise them, and accept them if you want to experience real love in a romantic relationship. Real love is not just a feeling. Real love is not fickle or self-serving or disposable. People are flawed. People are mean. People can hurt you.

If you cannot accept love from a perfect God, how can you accept love from an imperfect person?

"Love doesn't seek a return on its investment. Caring for someone to get something from them or to get them to change, isn't love. It's manipulation" (Jaron Myers).

As we grow spiritually and in our maturity, what it means to love someone or to be in love with someone evolves. For example, when I was in middle school, I was "in love" with someone who never even liked me back. No pity parties here. The point is that I thought that the limited interactions and trivial conversations I had with this person, combined with the fact that I found him attractive, had me thinking I loved him. Once again, I can't help but laugh at my twelve-year-old self. How silly that seems now. How silly that seemed when I got in to a long-term relationship. At the end of high school, I had my first real relationship, and boy, were we in love. At eighteen and nineteen years old, one year into our relationship, we had planned out when we would be married, how many kids we would have, what their names would be, and what kind of dog we were going to have. Those are some big plans for a couple of college freshmen. But love is seeing a future with someone, right? Love is sticking it out with one person forever, right? Love is falling into a comfortable and easy place with someone, right? Right, and also wrong. Love is not a plan. Love is not an obligation. Love is not easy.

Love is an attitude. It is a mindset. And sometimes, it is hard work. Find a solid Christian couple you know and ask them if they've ever had hard times. Ask them if there has ever been a time where they had to work at their relationship. The answer will be yes. Just like you have to wake up and choose to be intentional with how you love your friends and family, there will be days where you will have to choose love in a marriage. Sometimes it is easy to love the person you are with. There will be times when it is natural and it flows out of you and your relationship, but that is not constant. That is where God's love fills in the gaps. His love is the bridge where our love falls short.

Lesson 2: The Difference between Like, Love, and Infatuation

We have already discussed what love is. In relationships, love puts another person first. It builds up, it watches out for, it compromises, it corrects, and it forgives. Finding all of those things with someone who you can see a future with and who you are comfortable being yourself with, *that* is love. When it looks like God's love as described in the Bible, *that* is love.

But hey, if you're reading this book, there's a pretty good chance that you're single and that you are not in love at this moment. So, let us take a moment and figure out how exactly we get to a place of loving someone. A lot of things have to happen before you fall in love, but first and foremost, you need to have some initial reason that you like them. For the sake of identifying the difference between "liking" and being "infatuated," we will say that something had to first make you attracted to that person. Most often, initial attraction is based off of physical appearance, but sometimes it comes from other things—a sense of humor, similar interests, etc. But, a friend of mine explained it to me this way: how can you truly like a person and have feelings for a person if you don't even know them? Admiration from afar and nice, superficial conversations doesn't mean you're interested in being in a relationship with that person.

I've fallen victim to this firsthand. When I was in college I had a huge crush on this guy. I'm talking the debilitating type of crush where I couldn't even talk to this guy. I used to get pumped when he would just say "hi" to me in passing. I was head over heels in "like" with this guy. I could see a whole future. *Face-palm* I'm going to tell you right now, I'm not actually crazy. I had just been surrounded by crazy so long that it rubbed off on me a little. I didn't like this guy. I didn't know this guy. If someone asked me what I liked about him, I couldn't have given a reason besides the fact that he was attractive, and yet he was the focus of conversation with my roommate for *months*. That is what we call *infatuation*.

Being interested in someone and having feelings for someone may start the same way initially, but it ends up so very different. When you are getting to know someone that you are interested in, you want to learn about them. You spend time with them. You have conversations beyond what their favorite color is and what their favorite food is. You learn what is important to them, and if you find out that it is mutual, you continue from there. Feelings for someone aren't something to be afraid of, and they aren't a binding contract stating that you have to like that person forever. You have to work through them and see where they take you.

The bottom line is this: avoid infatuation. If you fall for the idea of being with a person and you never spend any time with them, or you can't hold a simple conversation with them, they're not real feelings. If you think you might like someone and want to get to know them better, go for it. Having feelings for someone is not a commitment to them. And, if you're lucky enough to have found love already—and you're not a mentor to any young single people—why are you reading a book written for single people? (I'm just curious)

Chapter 3
What Does the World Say about Relationships?

If you're like me and you grew up in the church, everything you learned about worldly relationships came from the media, observation, and whatever your non-Christian friends told you. Truthfully, what the media has told me and what I have observed line up pretty well with what people themselves have told me. But, hey, maybe you're a little more sheltered than I was (which was quite a bit) and you don't really understand dating outside of what I lovingly refer to as the Christian "bubble." No worries, we are all learning here.

The desire for relationships in the world is driven by most of the same things as relationships in the church. The key word there is "most." Believe it or not, people who are not religious experience the same kinds of wants and desires that we do. Profound, right? So what is driving these relationships? A desire to be loved. The hope to find someone to experience life with. Wanting a family. Those all sound pretty familiar don't they? Don't be fooled by that. There is one huge difference between worldly relationships and godly relationships (you know, besides the belief in God part). It's sex.

The world's current stance on sex outside of marriage is fairly new. For most of history, the face that the world put on was that sex should be only within the confines of marriage. I make the point that this is the "face" the world put on because we know that this was not necessarily what happened. It may have been what was expected or what was proper, but things were done in secret then just as they are now. Only now, the dialogue has changed. Rather than keeping it a secret that people sleep around and have sex outside of marriage, those lifestyles are promoted. They are not secret anymore. Women are empowered to have just as many one-night stands as men; people are told that they can't know if they are compatible until they have sex; open marriages are becoming more common. The openness that surrounds these matters didn't appear until around the 1960s. For thousands of years, premarital sex was a moral depravity, but in less than sixty years it has become a source empowerment and entertainment for people all across the globe.

What has pushed this change in attitude and action? Well, societal codes grow, shift, and change with time. That is normal. This change is a result of not one individual thing but a combination of many things. Birth control, equality, politics, young liberals, and (of course) the media have all worked together to spur this movement forward and to bring us to where we are today in the world: you can be whoever you want and sleep with whoever you want, whenever you want, wherever you want.

Our culture now perpetuates sex twenty-four hours a day, seven days a week. Music is filled with it. Television and movies not only talk about it but have been given a lot of liberty on what they can show now. Kids' shows have adult humor thrown into them to make them more entertaining for parents. There are commercials and posters everywhere of women in their underwear. People are flippant with their conversations and with their actions surrounding it. Pornography is easily accessible and easily stumbled upon. That is the culture we live in now. Sex is no big deal anymore.

In the church, we base our relationships off of loving Christ and working together to grow closer to Him and live in His will. What happens when you don't have God to be at the center of your relationships? Relationships become based on other things. Most, not all, relationships outside the bubble are based off of physical attraction and sexual chemistry. That is what initiates things and keeps them going until deeper bonds form. Some people base who they date off of what they can receive from the other, whether socially, emotionally, financially, or physically. Most people want to find someone that they just enjoy being with, someone that they have fun with.

> We all want to be loved, but we need to decide if we place our personal value in whether or not another person loves us.

Sex entangles relationships and bonds people together in a way that God only intended for marriage. When the world perpetuates a culture of meaningless sex and relationships based on sex, we end up with a lot of relationships and marriages that either end in true and utter heartbreak, or that are physically strong but emotionally dead. In all relationships, there is an attachment and a comfort that grows between two people. It is a natural feeling of safety and dependence. Sex adds a new level of intimacy between two people that makes their bond even closer and stronger. If that was meant for marriage, what happens when two people get together and are willing to create that closeness but not to commit to any type of serious relationship? Things get confusing. This is where that emotional turmoil—and eventual death—comes in. Sex never starts off as meaningless. Everyone makes a big deal of it at first. They want it to be with someone they love and who loves them back. And, why wouldn't they? The thing about sex is this: each person you have it with receives a claim to a piece of your heart, and hearts are generous things. In the beginning we give large portions of our heart to people expecting that they will stick around, and when they don't, there is a little less to give the next time around. If we continue on that path, eventually there is so little left to give that sex and relationships *do* become meaningless.

I think that it is easy to fall into a trap where you give so much of your heart away because you are sure that this time it is real; this time it is going to last. When it doesn't, you convince yourself that the next one will be "the one." That is a slippery slope. Sex is not something that should be given freely. It is not something that should be used to leverage commitment. It is a door that, no matter how hard you try or how much control you think you have, is not easy to close once it has been opened, and it can quickly become a driving force in your life. Here's the other thing: say you didn't rush into sex. Say you have been in a committed relationship and you think that sex is just the next step. Maybe you see yourselves heading toward marriage so there is no point in waiting. That's what the world would tell you to do.

There are no guarantees in relationships. There are not guarantees in engagements. By the world's standards, there aren't even guarantees in marriages anymore. All of it can end. I believe marriages are final and that is why that final bond created by sex is only for marriage, but out in the world, a lot of people see even marriage as something that you can choose to break off or to end. Why would you put yourself in such an emotionally and physically vulnerable position if you can't trust that the person will stick around afterward? If someone loves you but won't wait until you're married to have sex, do they really love you? Are they really committed to you? Do they value you the way you value them?

It can be tough existing in a world with beliefs so different from your own. I experience that on a daily basis at my job. The world pushes you to gratify your flesh; to have a good time now and worry about the consequences later. That may be fun and seem fulfilling in the moment, but in the long run? In the morning? After the dust settles? You'll probably stop seeing things with rose-colored glasses and you'll realize that doing whatever you want despite the consequences was the wrong choice. What is so great about auctioning off pieces of your heart for people to step on? What is so great about rolling the dice and hoping that wherever they land doesn't drastically alter the course of your life? What is so great about worldly relationships?

Lesson 3: It's All about Timing; Don't Rush the Process

Timing is so important in all relationships, but it seems like in the church we view relationships on an accelerated timeline. For example, when I went to my Christian college, it was guaranteed that by the end of the first week of each new year there would be freshmen who had never met before orientation staring new relationships. In essence, it went from "Hi nice to meet you, I'm from Pittsburg" on Wednesday to "where should we go on a date tonight" by the time classes started on Tuesday. I have tried so many times to understand the logic here and the truth is, there's no logic behind it. It is all hype from the new environment and the new people, but who can blame them? Most young Christians' choices have been limited to only the people in their youth group, so if they go to a Christian college, their dating pool goes from a few dozen to a few hundred. However, having more dating prospects does not mean that you should rush into anything.

A huge part of dating has to do with calculating the right time for things—when to ask someone out, when to be exclusive, when to kiss someone, when to say I love you, etc. If you act too early, the other person may not be ready, and if you act too late, the other person might move on without you. These things are the same whether you are a Christian or not. The difference is the accelerated timeline that I mentioned before. I hear stories *all the time* about couples who were married within less than twelve months from the day they met. That is crazy, and that terrifies me. I mean, that's great for those people (sometimes when you know, you know) but that is *for sure* not going to happen for everyone. How crazy is that though? I don't know how you feel like you know a person well enough in eleven months to choose to spend the rest of your life with them. I mean, if you went out into the world as a twenty-something and told someone that you were getting married to someone you met eight months ago, they would probably think you are either crazy or pregnant.

The other thing that someone may think when you get married quickly and you are a faithful Christian is that you are just getting married to have sex. I can't say that I would always argue with them. I can't say I haven't thought that about some people. Trust me I know that this is not the case for everyone (maybe not even most) that gets married fast and married young, but it's definitely not off the table for some people. Since waiting to have sex isn't a thing for most nonreligious people, it is not something that influences when they get married.

If you look at most relationships in the world, they move much slower than what we have become accustomed to seeing in church. I asked a friend of mine who didn't grow up in the bubble what she thought a reasonable relationship timeline was. Want to guess how long she thinks you should date before you get engaged/married? Two to three years. Heck, some Christians are married and on their second child by the time year three of their relationship rolls around. Some are already divorced.

Why such a long period of time before this step? You can still learn a lot of new things about a person two years into a relationship, and perhaps they are not great things or things you can live with. You know what else? Especially for those of us in our twenties, who you are, what you believe, and what you're passionate about can change drastically in the span of a couple years.

One danger of getting married young or too fast is that a year or two into the relationship, your partner could be someone almost completely different from who they were when you first met them. Change doesn't have to be a bad thing. Seeing how someone changes can make you more sure than ever that you belong together, or it could make you more sure than ever that you do not belong together. I've experienced firsthand how much someone can change in the span of a year or two. Your twenties are a time of drastic growth and that is something that is important to keep in mind in relationships. You have to remember that both people are growing and you need time to grow side by side before you know if you have a future grow-ing together.

The other thing that my friend suggested is that a good age to get married is twenty-six/twenty-seven. That is a popular opin-ion out in the world. People want the chance to become their own person, to explore and experience life before they are tied down to a marriage. While there are plenty of people who get married younger than that age and still have had fulfilling, adventurous, and successful marriages, it is an interesting thing to think about. There is no pres-sure to get married by the age of twenty-two. They have time to grow into full-blown adults *before* making vows they may not have valued or understood earlier in life.

All this to say, take your time. There is nothing wrong with taking the extra time to be sure that the person you are with is the person you want to marry. I think that there is something to be learned from the world here when it comes to relationships. We need to learn to slow down and take time to evaluate relationships. If we take the time to get to know people before we date them, we can avoid getting into relationships that we never really wanted. If we enjoy and value the time we have with someone rather than always looking forward to the end goal (marriage), we can have deeper and more meaningful relationships that prepare us for better marriages. Don't let the bubble pressure you or trick you into a relationship before you're sure you want it. You don't need the love story that starts out "we got married after six months of dating" and ends in "we got divorced after two years of marriage" all because you didn't really know the person you made vows to.

Chapter 4
What Does the Church Say about Relationships?

Not much. Now, on to chapter 5...

Okay, so that is about ½ joke and ½ serious. The truth of the matter is that relationships do not get talked about enough in church settings. Most of what young people are learning about relationships comes from the media and from their friends. The little that is learned about relationships inside the church is widely based off of observations instead of conversations. This is a huge problem. We learn a lot of stuff in life from observations, but if we never talk about what we see, we may find that we are interpreting things wrong.

And we wonder why so many Christians have a skewed view of relationships...

I had some phenomenal youth pastors and youth leaders in my life throughout middle and high school. They challenged me to know what I believed and taught me how to share that belief. But, going in to college, my basic understanding of relationships was as follows:

1. Don't have sex until you're married.
2. Set boundaries to prevent temptations.
3. Make sure you only date Christians.

So, looking at that list, it is obvious that we talked a bit about relationships. I'm sure there were other points made throughout my six years in youth group that didn't stick. However, as far as I can remember, the conversation about relationships was always focused on the "purity" aspect of the relationship. Don't misunderstand me; that discussion is *essential* to have with young people, but it is not the only conversation we should be having. There is so much more to having a God-centered, spiritually healthy relationship than remaining pure.

There really is no blame to be placed on any one pastor, mentor, or church. The blame has to be placed on the attitude of church as a whole. Why don't we talk about relationships more? Is it because we don't know how to? Is it because we don't want to step on anyone's toes? Is it because we don't know what to say? I would suggest that a few of the reasons we don't talk about relationships very often is that there is a lack of experience, a lack of awareness, and a lack of resources.

There are so many people in the church who fall into relationships at a young age that happen to work out in the end. If those people end up in places of influence, they may find themselves lacking in the experience and the wisdom required to teach young people how to go about relationships. This also can perpetuate the "one right way to have a relationship" attitude that plagues the church. It's hard to teach something you've never seen, heard, or experienced before.

We could also attribute this gap in teaching to an inattentiveness to the issue itself. If a teacher is unaware of holes in a student's learning, he or she is unable to address the problem. This is the same concept. Relationships are often loud and in your face (metaphorically speaking). You can see them. They get talked about and celebrated, but because they are visible, they can distract you from the people who are not fitting into that mold. If you forget that there are people who choose another path (or who have life take them on another path), you may forget to celebrate that path with them. And, perhaps, because they are on a less celebrated path, young people are afraid to or don't know how to ask for help in relationships.

Finally, I think that there is a lack of materials to help pastors and mentors foster a healthy attitude toward relationships in the church. Whether that means there is a lack of godly couples who want to pour into the lives of young people, or there is a lack of literature to combat a lack of knowledge, something is missing. It is our job as a church to step up and fill in the gaps that are allowing our young people to slip through to adulthood with wrong and shallow ideas of what their relationships should look like.

One of the most important things that we need to understand and teach is that every relationship is different. There is no specific formula for how to have a successful relationship or for how to have a relationship that leads to marriage (no matter how intently sister so-and-so insists there is). There are, however, guidelines that we can be providing to young people—teenagers and young adults—that will help them fall into fewer relationships that were headed nowhere to begin with or that end in utter heartbreak.

Lesson 4: Your Dating Requirements Need to Be More Than "Is He/She a Christian?"

I wouldn't call myself the kind of person to have a "type." I have always found myself crushing on people with a wide variety of looks, interests, talents, and hobbies. That being said, my list of "must-haves" when considering if I would want to date someone was quite small for my entire adolescence. Like, really small. The first and the last box on my checklist was

☐   Does he love Jesus?

If I could check that off, then I figured he was good enough and that things would work out. Well, well, well, fifteen-year-old me, the joke is on you. The fact that someone both knows and loves Jesus doesn't guarantee anything in relationships. Knowing Christ is the first step, but there are a lot of other things that go into a successful and long-lasting relationship.

It is easy to call yourself a Christian. "Christian" can be just a word. In fact, there are young people in relationships all over the country where one person is a Christian and the other has taken on the name of a Christian just so that they can be in the relationship. That should be an immediate red flag. If you're not sure if they are the real deal or faking it, look at the person's life.

"So, every healthy tree bears good fruit, but the diseased tree bears bad fruit… Thus you will recognize them by their fruits" (Matt. 7:17, 20, ESV).

If you find yourself in a relationship with someone who calls themselves a Christian, but whose life bears no spiritual fruit, they are not living the Christ-centered life that we are all called to live. And, if they are not living a Christ-centered life, you should not be in a relationship with them. If you come to the conclusion that the person you are dating or are looking to date is an actual Christian, that is great, but you're not out of the woods yet.

When we talk about what kind of things you need to look for in someone you might want a relationship with, we are talking about things that are much deeper than following the same God. You both need to desire and seek after what God has for you individually and as a couple. You need to agree on how far is too far, and if you have different opinions on where the boundaries belong, you need to agree to stay within boundaries where you *both* feel comfortable. You need to figure out if your callings can coincide. If one of you is called to the mission field and the other would never leave home, it's probably not meant to be. Or, if one of you knows that God is preparing you for a life that drops everything and moves on a dime, and He is preparing the other for a long-term vocation in one place, you may find that someone has to sacrifice their calling for the sake of the relationship.

Don't sacrifice what God has called you to for a relationship that may not have been God ordained in the first place.

Another important part of your checklist is knowing what you believe. Not just the basics, but other important things like the gifts of the Spirit, homosexuality, women in ministry, drinking alcohol, etc. You need to decide for yourself in which of these things you must remain steadfast in your convictions and which ones have some room for compromise. You don't always have to have identical beliefs in all of these things, but knowing them ahead of time is important. Why? Well, when you get into a relationship and begin to look toward marriage, these should be things that have already been talked about. In fact, I would suggest that these are some things you may want to find out about a person while you are still just friends. That way, you don't get into premarital counseling and find out you have some opposing theology that you have determined there is no compromise to.

Lesson 5: You Don't Have to Marry the First Person You Date

The church has set up this false idea that you have to court rather than date and that, if you do it right, the first person you're in a relationship with will be the one that you marry. Whether or not anyone says that aloud, it is an attitude that is more common than you think. I know that growing up I felt like we always talked so highly about people who married their first boyfriend or girlfriend, but we didn't really acknowledge those who had to date a few people to find the right one. The attitude was that an ended relationship was a complete failure and waste of time. Or, a lot of the talk among those who were single was that they only wanted to date the person they would marry—skip all of the messy stuff in between. I am here to tell you that I did not marry the first person I ever dated, and that I do not consider that relationship a failure in the slightest. No, it did not work out, and yes, it ended for good reason, but I learned so much. The "messy" stuff is so much more important than you realize.

Dating someone that I did not end up marrying taught me a whole list of things about myself and about relationships in general. First off, it got me out of the mindset that I simply needed to date a Christian and everything else would fall into place. Denominational differences are not talked about very often, and yet they can put a huge strain on relationships. But, having the opportunity to date someone with different theology forced me to evaluate what I believe and why I believe it. If I had married him, let's just say that we would have had a lot of very…loud…discussions about our faith and about what to teach our children.

Dating also helped me determine what it takes to have a healthy relationship and what I would expect out of someone I am in a relationship with. It is very easy to build up in your head an idea of what a relationship with someone would be like. It is easy to fabricate what a marriage would be like. You can project what you want or what you think you should want out of a relationship onto people, and when it comes about in real life, it is not all you hoped it would be. What happens when you never date someone because they don't fit the type of person in your head that you want to marry? When you finally find someone who fits the ideal and you realize that things aren't as peachy as you imagined, but you waited so long for this guy (or girl) that you feel stuck? I pray that you don't go into a marriage feeling stuck. I pray that you don't trick yourself into loving and marrying someone so that you don't have to go through the dating process again or so that you can say you married your first love.

Marriage is serious business. It is not something to be entered into lightly. The bottom line is that some people do find the right person on the first try and most people do not. We need to begin to celebrate both paths equally. Both ways are good and acceptable. Both ways can end in happy and loving marriages that last. The unspoken and unaddressed attitude in the church that marrying the first person you ever have a relationship with is the "right way" to do things needs to die. God has got your back. He knows what relationships are and are not meant to last. He knows exactly how to use each one to help you grow into the person He desires you to be.

———

Let me tell you the story of the twenty-one-year-old college senior. You see, she was getting ready to graduate from Christian college as a young, single female, and every time she turned a corner there was another church person who was trying to influence her into a relationship with someone she didn't want or was questioning why she hadn't found someone to marry yet. She didn't feel too confident after a while. She started to question God's plan, but she eventually (re)discovered that God's plan is way better than her own. You see, if she listened to all of those people, she would probably be in an unhappy relationship. Maybe she would have convinced herself she loved one of those "ideal" guys enough to marry him. Maybe she would come to her senses before she invested too much time and energy into a relationship she didn't want in the first place.

There are a lot of maybes and what-ifs when we listen to what people say. People are flawed and foolish; therefore, their plans and opinions are often flawed and foolish. God's ways are so far above and beyond our own. Don't be the person who ends up unhappy and far from God's plan because he listened to what people had to say. Be the person filled with joy and who is walking in God's will because he decided that God's way was better than his own or than someone else's. It took me time to get there. I still on occasion default back to thinking I'm somehow off track from where I should be because those attitudes can be so pervasive in a church environment, but God always pulls me back. He always reminds me how worth it this will all be in the end.

If you are single and have experienced those kinds of pressures from people in the church like I have, don't sit quietly and accept that. Challenge what people are saying to you. Be confident in your singleness. Change how you think, then change how your church thinks, and eventually change how we all think.

Chapter 5
What Does the Bible Say about Relationships?

It should be obvious to us to look to the Bible for relationship advice, shouldn't it? It should be our first place to run to when we have questions or run into trouble, and yet it always seems to be our last resort. We run to our parents, our friends, our pastor. We read books and we listen to music, all before we look to the word of God. It gives us all kinds of instruction on how to have healthy and godly relationships, but it sits on the sidelines, and when all of the other players are exhausted, it is called onto the field as a last resort. Then, when it has the right answers, we all act amazed at how great it is, and we act as though it wasn't available to us the whole time! We need to start treating the Word of God as the MVP rather than a last round draft pick.

The Bible gives us a lot of advice on how to have relationships as well as many warnings on what to be careful of in relationships. If you look at Paul's letters to the early churches, many of them include instructions on relationships, marriages, and living pure lives, but Paul isn't the only one who addressed this topic. We can find writings about relationships all through the Old and New Testaments. So, it is obvious that looking for help in relationships is no new problem. Let's start with this question: How do I know when I can start dating?

Easy to answer, harder to accept and carry out. God's timing is everything. The question of whether to be in a relationship now or be single all falls down to that. God knows our hearts. He knows our desires. We've already talked about how God does not wish to withhold good things from us. Psalm 37:4 says to "Delight yourself in the Lord, and he will give you the desires of your heart." (ESV) When we look at that verse, we focus most often on the part where God gives us our desires. How typical of us to only focus on what we get out of the deal. What we need to focus on is the first part. We should delight in the Lord. That means not becoming anxious or discouraged with that we desire and do not have, but finding contentment and joy in what He has already given us. When we delight in the Lord (when we stop seeking other desires above Him), He will give us the desires of our hearts.

Sometimes we try to circumnavigate God's will to make it to our desires in our own timing. What a dangerous game that is. In the end, making your own plans that go around God's plans will only result in hurting yourself. God's plans are final and they will not be put on hold for the sake of someone who is trying to get around them or ignore them.

"Many are the plans in the mind of a man, but it is the purpose of the Lord that will stand" (Prov. 19:21, ESV).

The problem when it comes to dating or being single is whether or not our hearts are in the right place. *Why* you want to be in a relationship is far more important than if you *can* or *should* be in a relationship. If you are looking to fill an empty space in your heart, stay single. If you are being pressured into a relationship you aren't sure you want, stay single. If you want a relationship because everyone around you is in one, stay single. These are all wrong motivations to be in a relationship. The only person that should be filling an empty space in your heart is God. A relationship that fills empty space in your heart takes away part of your heart when it ends, but when your heart is already filled with Christ, any relationship can only add to your heart. And if it does end, it can't take a piece of your heart because it was already filled with Christ to begin with.

If you're being pressured into a relationship, don't just give in to what other people think you are supposed to be doing. People create a lot of hype around situations without thinking through the finer points or the possible consequences. And the truth is, if people are pressuring you into something that you are not ready for or something that you don't want, you should question the role you allow them to play in your life. When it comes to looking for a relationship just to fit in to your group of friends or just to feel like you're not missing out, check your heart. Think about the other person's heart. This relationship may not be a joke or a filler to them. Besides, having friends in relationships provides a prime opportunity for you to observe what to do and what not to do in a relationship.

Longing and desire are powerful things, and it is a difficult thing when your deepest desires do not line up with God's will in the moment. The trick is not allowing your desires to have more power in your life than you allow God to have. In her book, *Passion & Purity*, Elisabeth Elliot presents an idea of God's answer to our longing that most of us are probably unfamiliar with. She writes, "My heart was saying, 'Lord, take away this longing, or give me that for which I long.' The Lord was answering, 'I must teach you to long for something better.'" So often we ask God why He isn't giving us the things that we ask for and the things that we desire. There may not be a simple black-and-white answer: remove the desire or satisfy it. The answer may be something in between: change my desire. When we look at this type of situation and miss this third outcome, we end up missing an opportunity for Him to teach us to desire something else even more—something else that is even greater.

If you're asking yourself whether it is an okay time for you to date or not, begin by looking inwardly. Are you delighting in the Lord? Are you seeking your desires or God's desires? Are you making your own plans, or submitting to God's? Are you trying to fill an emptiness in your heart with something other than Christ?

Does the Bible Say I Should Be Single or Married?

At a quick glance, you will find the answer is that it encourages both. Singleness is meant for everyone up to a certain point. I mean, we aren't born married are we? So, yes. You should be single. And maybe someday you will be married, but let's look at some scripture for each lifestyle.

Paul teaches us a lot about singleness and marriage in his letters. One particular place where we find a lot of information on this topic is in 1 Corinthians 7. In verses 1–5, Paul writes that men and women should marry in order to flee the temptation of sexual immorality. Right after that, in verse 7, he writes, "I wish that all were as I myself am. But each has his own gift from God, one of one kind and one of another." (ESV) It is safe to say that when Paul wishes "all were as [he]," he means that he wishes all people would remain single. A single life makes it much easier to follow the call of God and to uproot life to move where He wills. However, Paul is no fool. He knows that not all people are called to a life of singleness. He actually speaks of celibacy as a gift from God, or a gift of the Spirit, that is not for everyone. He continues on to repeat his warning against the temptation of sexual immorality, saying that "if they cannot exercise self-control, they should marry. For it is better to marry than to burn with passion." (ESV)

I know that Paul seems to go back and forth a bit there on what he is saying, so I am going to break it down for you. Singleness allows you flexibility where marriage does not. However, singleness is not a mandate from God. Purity is. While some people are called to a life of celibacy, others are not so...lucky. Rather than live life as a single who is constantly tempted toward or constantly succumbing to sexual immorality, get married.

Paul was obviously called to the single life in his ministry. He believed that Christ's return was coming quickly and that the things that will pass away (such as marriage) should be put aside to further the call of Christ. This is why he is so heavy-handed on the advice toward being single. "Yet those who marry will have worldly troubles, and I would spare you that." "From now on, let those who have wives live as though they had none." (ESV) It is true that being married brings new elements into your life that can complicate it. It is also true that marriage has the potential to limit what you are willing to do for the great commission.

Don't be discouraged! There is still hope! While Paul promotes the benefits of singleness, Solomon shows us pictures of love in the Old Testament. The entire book of songs written by Solomon is a collection of poems written between a man and his wife. Its simple inclusion in the canon of scripture supports the practice of marriage. Solomon also writes this Ecclesiastes:

> Two are better than one, because they have a good reward for their toil. For if they fall, one will lift up his fellow. But woe to him who is alone when he falls and has not another to lift him up! Again, if two lie together, they keep warm, but how can one keep warm alone? And though a man might prevail against one who is alone, two will withstand him—a threefold cord is not quickly broken. (Eccles. 4:9–12, ESV)

This is another popular wedding passage that has meaning in both platonic and romantic relationships. In all circumstances, it is important to have someone you are close to. They can defend you and help you through life. It is a simple fact that people are stronger when they are united with someone else. There is strength in numbers. In some seasons of life, our second person is a friend or family member. That isn't a bad thing, but friends and family often grow distant whether it is emotionally or geographically. Who better to watch your back, lift you up, and go through life with than a spouse? I'm not saying that you should run out and find a spouse right now for the sake of finding someone to follow this scripture with. I am saying that once you get to that place, a marriage is (or should be) a built in solution to this. It comes back to that last line "a threefold cord is not quickly broken." A marriage that is rooted in God always has someone to fall back on—a spouse and God or just God. There may be troubles, but they will not break you if God is the foundation. So, I would say that this passage talks about marriage as beneficial.

Another important thing to consider is that when God made Adam and Eve, he made them husband and wife. If that wasn't His plan for all of creation, why would He have started us off in that way?

The Bible presents paths toward lives of singleness and of marriage. The real question has to do with what you are called to in this season of life. I cannot give you an answer for what the future holds for you. I can offer you this—to be single is to be free. Free to follow God's will and free to fulfill his call. You do not need to rush into marriage because you think it is what you are "supposed to do." If you're trying to figure out what stage you're at, just talk to God. Seek out what He wants for you. He's not going to ignore you as you try to seek out His will. That is not who God is. You will just need to learn to listen for what He is trying to tell you.

How Do I Know Who to Date?

There is this verse in 2 Corinthians, maybe you have heard it before: "Do not be unequally yoked with unbelievers." We just established that idea in lesson 4—do not get into a relationship with someone who does not believe in Christ like you believe in Christ. But what does it mean to be unequally yoked? When two animals are yoked together, they are connected and harnessed to each other. They must work together at the same pace in order to reach a destination or accomplish a goal. If one animal is stronger than the other, two things can happen. The first is that the stronger animal will try to compensate for the weaker one, bearing more of the burden and in turn dragging the other animal along beside it. The second is that the stronger animal has to slow down to the pace and ability of the weaker animal. I know we all *love* being compared to livestock, but this metaphor can be applied to more than just a relationship between believers and nonbelievers. It can also be applied to relationships between believers. "But the Bible specifically says unbelievers!" This is where we begin to talk about the letter of the law versus the spirit of the law. The letter of the law tells us not to be in a relationship with unbelievers. The spirit of the law tells us not to be in a relationship with anyone who will slow us down or deter us from our goal. That means that if someone is a Christian, but they are not helping you to grow spiritually, you may be unequally yoked.

One of the best physical and visual representations I have ever seen of this concept involves two people and a sturdy chair. The two people face each other while one person stands on the chair and the other stands on the floor. They simultaneously try to pull the other person to the same level at which they are standing. Every time the person on the floor wins. It is nearly impossible to pull someone up to the level of the chair, just as it is impossible to force someone into a new level of commitment and belief. When that happens, the only way for two people to end up on the same level is for the person who is higher/stronger to lower themselves to the other person's level, effectively stunting their own spiritual growth.

One important thing to mention here is that there is no standing still in this matter. You cannot simply continue as you are and wait for the other person to catch up to you. You are either moving toward God or away from Him. Being unequally yoked, whether with a believer or an unbeliever, can be detrimental to your spiritual health. We should be growing and learning as much as we can, rather than slowing down to pull a boyfriend or girlfriend along.

Besides figuring out whether the person you are dating or hoping to date is as serious about their faith as you are, you also need to evaluate the type of person that they are. Is he living the type of life that the Bible tells him to? Is he kind, patient, good, gentle, and faithful? Is she filled with love, peace, joy, patience, and self-control (Gal. 5:22–23)? Does he become anxious, or does he rely on the Lord (1 Pet. 5:7)? Is she full of deceit, or does she fear the Lord (Prov. 31:30)? Is he quick to get angry? Is she slow to listen (James 1:19)? We need to look at the characteristics described in the Bible to see if the person we desire to be with is living, or working toward living, that type of lifestyle. Someone who is not trying to be better and live more in these things daily is not someone that you should be with. And, hey, while you're checking on those biblical characteristics in their life, check out your own. Make sure that you are living a life representative of Christ and the call that He has given you.

Chapter 6
What Does the Bible Say about You?

The Bible is a never-ending well of knowledge, and when we open it, that knowledge flows from it and into our lives. It teaches us about Christ, about the heart of God, about friendships, about relationships, about loss, about joy, and it teaches us about ourselves. What you think and believe about yourself is probably more important than you realize. The way that we view ourselves has the ability to make or break our relationships, friendships, careers, and education.

So, how do you view yourself? Do you often succumb to the pictures other people paint of you? Do you accept their assessments of your character and your worth without question? I hope not. People are flawed and they make flawed judgments. There is this thing that we do as humans where we listen to what people say about us, true or untrue, we believe it, and then we become it. There have been plenty of times in my life where I have had people tell me things about myself (or imply things about me) so many times that I started to believe it. I'll give you two examples.

The first has to do with my calling from God. I know for sure that a piece of my calling has me involved in leading worship, and I had never really questioned that until I came across an opportunity to audition for a traveling worship team and didn't make the cut three years in a row. Sure, no one ever told me flat out that I wasn't good enough or didn't have whatever they thought a worship leader needed to have, but that is what the situation implied: there were other people who were better, other people who fit the profile better.

For a while after that, I began to question that piece of my calling. That was something I had never done until human voices were added to the mix, and it turns out, people were wrong and I needed only to listen to what God had to say. Besides, that opportunity turned out to be part of my own plans and not God's plans, so the fact that I was not chosen had nothing to do with my abilities and everything to do with being where God wanted me to be.

The other example I will give you has to do with relationships. I have the type of personality where I get along better with members of the opposite sex, and more times than not, people see how comfortable I am with my guy friends and assume that it means that I like them as more than just friends. While I know well enough now how to discern my own feelings toward someone, when I was fourteen for some reason I thought that other people knew better. There was this guy—we will call him Mark—who I had known my whole life. He felt like family to me, but other people saw how I interacted with him and interpreted it as me flirting with him. So, they had to butt in, and they asked me if I liked him. It went something like this:

No, I don't like Mark.
You totally do!
Not that I am aware of.
But, you guys would be so cute together!
I mean I guess so.
He probably likes you too
Do you really think so?
Definitely! See? You do like him!
Okay, maybe I do a little.
You guys are totally going to get married!

Did you catch that? I know it sounds silly, but I actually got convinced into liking someone, and I would venture a guess that I am not the only person whose friends have talked her into liking someone or at least liking the idea of someone. Whether it was due to some crazy need to feel like I had something to offer, or my need to please people, or some other issue about myself I had not yet discovered, I found myself focusing for a couple months on trying to begin a relationship with this person who I hadn't even come to my own conclusion about and in the end realized I never had real feelings for. Let that speak to the power that your words can have over people.

When it has to do with your purpose, your calling, your self-worth, and your relationships, *don't trust what people say!* I know not all people give bad advice. I have an amazing group of godly people in my life who I know for a fact give me wisdom from heaven and who spend time in God's presence to gain that wisdom, but I don't blindly take whatever they say as a fact (no matter how many times they have been right in the past). I take what they say, I look to God's word, and I pray about it before I believe it. You see, that annoying thing that people used to tell you growing up, that "it doesn't matter what people think/say about you," is actually true. What really matters is what Christ says about you. When you become confident in who your Heavenly Father created you to be, opposing opinions don't seem to hurt as much.

How do you know what God says about you? You look to His word. I don't care how long you have been in the church or how many times you have read the Bible, there is always something new to learn from God's word.

God Knew You and Loved You before You Were Even Born

This is a concept that is not foreign to you if you grew up in the church. We know that God is omniscient, or all-knowing, and that His knowledge is not limited to the present but transcends time. That means that before God even spoke light into existence, He knew you. He knew you and He desired for you to know Him. Ephesians 1:4–5 tells us that God "chose us in him *before the foundation of the world,* (emphasis mine) that we should be holy and blameless before him. In love he predestined us for adoption as sons through Jesus Christ, according to the purpose of his will." (ESV) There are no surprises with God. When you were born, He already knew who you would become. When you make a mistake and sin, He knew it would happen. When you hit rock bottom, He saw it coming from a long, long way off.

We often make the mistake Adam and Eve did when they hid from God in the garden. We act like we can cover up our sin and pretend God doesn't know about it when He knew it would happen before anyone else did. But God's grace goes so far beyond what we expect or deserve. God knew that we would be sinners before the foundation of the world, and yet He chose to love us. He chose to make a way for us to have forgiveness. He chose to adopt us into His family by His Spirit in spite of all the wrong things we would do.

When God called the prophet Jeremiah, He spoke to him and said, "Before I formed you in the womb I knew you, and before you were born I consecrated you; I appointed you a prophet to the nations" (Jer. 1:5, ESV). I'm going to let you in on a little secret here: God may have been speaking directly to Jeremiah in this verse, but that statement was not and is not just about Jeremiah. Do you think that God only knew Jeremiah before he was born? Do you think that Jeremiah was the only person God appointed to ministry before he was born? Of course not! God planned for you, He formed you, He loved you, and He appointed you long before you ever took your first breath.

It is an important thing for you to understand that God chose you and chose to love you a long time ago. When you accept that godly love that surpasses time and understanding, it changes the way that you view yourself. You begin to see value in your life in ways that you had not noticed before.

You Were Created Precisely and Purposefully

This should be obvious to us, shouldn't it? We know nothing that God ever does is an accident, and yet we often question why we were created and why He has placed us in our particular situation. We find imperfection in what God Himself sat, imagined, and set into motion. Why do we do this? How do we come up with these ideas that are directly in contrast with His word? Psalm 139:13 says, "For you created my inmost being; you knit me together in my mother's womb." (ESV) I do not knit, but I know that knitting is a precise craft. It takes focus and it takes skill. It is no coincidence that we see this image of precision and concentration when talking about how God created us. It implies the specific kind of care and attention to detail that was used when you were formed.

That intentionality in our creation is nothing new. When we look back to the creation of the world, we can see that intentionality in the creation of man. Before God created man, He created many things: sky and water, land and sea, light and darkness, plants and animals. With each of these things, God spoke and they existed. But when God made man, He did not simply speak.

"Then the Lord God formed the man of dust from the ground and breathed into his nostrils the breath of life, and the man became a living creature" (Gen. 2:7, ESV). My pastor has put it this way:

> Not with His voice, but with His (metaphorical) hands He formed us. With His breath, He gave us life. Why would God change His pattern of creation when He came to creating us? We know that God's words would have been powerful enough to create man, but the intimacy—the intentionality—that goes along with God forming man and breathing life into him was meant to be different. It was meant to give us pause. To breathe life into someone is to be close to them, to be personal with them. When God created man, He created him out of the desire for a close and intimate relationship with him. He could have grouped us in with the creation of the animals, but instead He set us apart. We were created in such a personal way because God wanted us to have a personal relationship with Him. (Rev. David Fisher)

God Wants You to Be Filled with Joy and to Live a Full Life

News flash! God does not want you to live a sad, poor, uneventful, dry, lonely, and empty life! In fact, I don't know where we got this idea that God wants to give us just enough to get by. Just enough money to pay the bills; just enough happiness to keep us from depression; just enough of His Spirit to keep us believing. If you really believe those things about God, I'm not sure that we are serving the same one. I serve a God that wants to see His people thrive. He wants them to be filled with joy and with love and with the power of the Holy Spirit.

> Which of you, if your son asks for bread, will give him a stone? Or if he asks for a fish, will give him a snake? If you, then, though you are evil, know how to give good gifts to your children, how much more will your Father in heaven give good gifts to those who ask him! (Matt. 7:9–11, NIV)

My parents don't enjoy seeing me sad or struggling. In fact, odds are that if I'm crying my mom is crying with me. They are good parents. They love me and they have always taken care of me. Whether or not you have had good parents, you probably know what good parents look like. If the whole world had a vote and agreed on two people to be named the best parents to ever exist, they would still only be ranked on earthly standards. Our Heavenly Father is so good, so loving, and so kind that He has His own category. If earthly parents do not want their children to suffer, why would God?

Sometimes we get into this mindset where we cannot ask God for anything more because we need to simply be grateful for what we already have. While it is true that we need to thank God for what He has given us, we can always ask for more. To have more—money, time, influence, etc.—is to have more to give. In fact, God desires to give us more. He wants to bless us so that we can in turn bless others. What God does *not* want to do is make all of us Christians rich and famous so we can keep it all for ourselves. When God blesses us and fills us, it is so that we can overflow into the lives of other people. That is where this idea of fullness and prosperity comes from.

In the middle of my college career, I realized that I was not seeking the full life that God desired for me to have. It was then that I rediscovered and took hold of John 10:10 and began applying it to my life: "The thief comes only to steal and kill and destroy. I came that they may have life and have it abundantly." (ESV) God not only desires that you have life, He also desires that you have an abundant life. A life that bears fruit. A life that takes care of others and has more than enough left over to take care of yourself. It is out of our blessings that we bless others. It is out of our joy in Christ that we spread joy to the world.

"As each has received a gift, use it to serve one another, as good stewards of God's varied grace" (1 Pet. 4:10, ESV).

It is very possible that you have read all of the passages I just talked about before. It is also very possible that when you read them, you didn't dwell on what they said and you didn't hold onto them. When we are little we are taught to hide God's word in our hearts (Ps. 119:11). Take these truths from scripture and hide them in your heart so that when the enemy tries to pry his way into your life by way of your insecurities, loneliness, and doubts, you have the ammunition you need to fight him off. Remember, Jesus fought temptation with scripture. Why shouldn't you?

While the message of God's word never changes, its emphasis shifts depending on the stage of life you are in. In this time of being single, allow God to teach you to see yourself and your life in the ways that He sees you. God does not make mistakes, and He doesn't want you to live some mundane life. He wants you to be vibrant. He wants you to thrive. Does that mean that there won't be hard times? Absolutely not! There will be hard times. There will be sad times. There will be times where you may not know what is next, but those are the times that build faith. God is always in control. He is a God of order and not of chaos. He has a plan, and He truly does desire to see you succeed.

"'For I know the plans I have for you,' declares the Lord, 'plans to prosper you and not harm you, plans to give you hope and a future'" (Jer. 29:11, ESV).

Chapter 7
What Do You Want?

We have already addressed this question a little bit up to this point, but I feel like it is something that we need to dive deeper into, because knowing what you want in life and in relationships is important. Why is it important? There are a number of reasons, but I would argue that the most prominent is that going into any occasion blindly is a risky game. Spiritual, emotional, and situational blindness all can leave you open to attacks and intrusions that could easily knock you off course. Have you ever heard the term "blindsided"? This term originates from athletics but has made its way into language as a common idiom. When you are blindsided, you are hit, knocked over, or otherwise deterred by something that came from somewhere outside of your range of vision. When we walk through life blindly, it is easy for us to be blindsided. That seems like a pretty obvious concept, doesn't it? And yet, it happens all of the time.

How do we overcome this blindness? Sometimes it isn't easy. Sometimes it requires work to force off the tendencies to walk blindly through our everyday life. You must take the time to unwrap the layers upon layers of bandages that have bound your eyes closed for so long. Other times it is simply opening your eyes to go from asleep to awake and making a decision, a choice, to see. This is a lesson that you need to learn not only in relationships but also in life. Determining what you want and what you expect out of situations and out of people helps you be better prepared and make better choices.

As much as I would like to help you figure out what you want in life, we are focusing on singleness and on relationships, so I'll stick to that. And, since singleness comes before being in a relationship, we will begin there.

What Do You Want out of Being Single?

I guess that a more important first question would be do you even want to be single? It is a valid question. There are some people who really want to be in a season of singleness and there are some people who are in a season of singleness simply biding their time until the right person comes around. Either way, you should figure out what you want to come out of this period in your life.

I told you before that singleness is freedom. It gives you space to move and grow on your own. There are so many things that can be learned in a season of singleness. If you are a person who desires to be single right now, it is undoubtedly because you have other things you want to focus on. Perhaps you want to focus on your career or on ministry without the added distraction of a relationship. It could be that between school, athletics, and after-school activities you don't have the time right now. Maybe you simply need to take the time to focus on your relationship with God. Whatever it is, it is a conscious decision that there is something more important at this time in your life than being in a relationship.

That is an entirely acceptable attitude to have. The beauty of being single is that you have the time to focus on other things that are *good* things in your life. Yes, being in a relationship can be good and it can be beneficial to you, but it can also be time-consuming and physically and emotionally draining. Being healthy is a good thing. Thinking about your career is a good thing. Spending time with your family is a good thing. The truth is that there are only so many hours in a day, and if you are in a full and busy season of your life, the choice to remain single is likely a choice with the aim of bringing balance into your life.

However, not all of us want to be single at the moment. Sometimes, we find ourselves in situations where we feel emotionally and spiritually ready to be in a relationship but there's no one that fits what we are looking for. Or maybe there is someone that fits the mold, but they don't feel the same way, or the other person is the one making the choice to be single in this season. Maybe you're wanting to be in a relationship but you're wanting it for the wrong reasons. Been there, experienced all of that.

Rather than pine after someone you can't have or wallow in the fact that there isn't anyone suitable at the moment, you need to look at singleness in the way that the people who choose singleness look at it. Face it as an opportunity and not an obstacle. Face it as a teachable moment rather than a failed endeavor. There is no reason to sit around feeling sorry for yourself for not dating someone. I've found myself on multiple occasions in the past sitting in my room feeling sorry for myself because there was a boy that I had liked for a really long time that didn't like me back. Sure, it hurts when we put so much emotional stock into some relationship that we are hoping for, but life goes on. There are so many other things in life that are bigger than relationships, and the sooner you grasp this concept, the sooner things will start to seem different.

The God that I serve is a God of order. He is a God who makes what is broken whole. He is a God who provides beyond just what I need. He is a God that, in spite of the many, many, many human problems He deals with that seem bigger than this young woman's relationship status, still hears her and cares about what is going on in her heart. I can't say there is any way to convince yourself you are content or happy being single when you aren't. I can say there is a God who I can be content and happy to serve, and that when I find those things in Him, they begin to flow over in to other areas of my life.

This idea that God can use your singleness to help you grow emotionally and spiritually gets lost in the hoopla of finding some-one to marry. His desire is that a relationship enhance your life, not define your life. You need to be your own person before you give someone else the influence that they gain from a relationship with you. Becoming your own person takes time. It takes *this* time of being single and allowing God to move in you.

Whether you are single because you want to be single or because you're "stuck" being single, it is time to decide what you want to get out of this season. Do you want to really find out the kind of person you are on your own? Do you need to take time to breathe and refocus on your goals? Do you need to simply spend more time loving Jesus? Whenever you start to think about the fact that you are single, start asking yourself those questions. Truthfully, if you don't have a firm grasp on who you are, can't balance your time well, and aren't seeking after Jesus like you should be, you are not going to make a very good boyfriend or girlfriend to someone. I'm not looking for perfection, but no one wants to date an emotional and spiritual mess.

What Do You Want out of a Relationship?

Knowing what you want or expect out of a relationship is just as important as knowing what you want to get out of being single. Relationships can be a big deal and can be surrounded by some big decisions. Knowing what you expect and what you want ahead of time can help you make better decisions about who to be in a relationship with in the first place. Anyone who has experienced it will tell you that it is no fun getting into a relationship and realizing months or years into it that you're two people with different ideas about where the relationship is going.

I was in a relationship for a year and a half before I discovered something that was a deal-breaker. Part of the reason it took so long to figure it out is that the topic didn't come up, and the other part is that I didn't realize that it was something that was important to me until it finally did come up. In other words, I didn't know what I wanted from a person I was in a relationship with. I didn't know what was important to me. Learn from me and from other people around you. Use your time as a single to really figure out what you want from the relationship itself and from the other person.

Another important question to consider is, what are you expecting to get emotionally from a relationship? This is something that is so incredibly important that I know people ignore and overlook on a constant basis. Relationships are emotional things. They make their way into the deepest depths of our hearts and their effects have a way of lingering there even after relationships end. I'm not just talking about romantic relationships here either. I'm talking about all relationships. Things that have happened with friends, with family members, and with exes. The effects of those relationships take root deep within us and can change how we relate to people long after they end.

It is easy for us to allow the past to dictate what we expect emotionally out of a relationship. Time and time again I see people, young and not-so-young, enter into relationships where they aim to fill an emotional void in their life. A void left by a physically or emotionally absent parent. A void created from not having close and dependable friends. A void made when a relationship ends and that person takes a piece of your heart with them. A void that the media has slowly carved into their heart then convinced them they have to fill. Relationships are emotional things.

When we try to fill a space in our lives that has become empty or void with something that is as fickle and as fleeting as emotions, we set ourselves up for failure in a big way. Any empty spaces in your heart or your life need to be filled with Jesus before you try to add something like a relationship to the mix.

Christ is a permanent solution to your emptiness and your loneliness.

People are temporary bandages that when removed rip away more of you than they ever fixed. Christ, therefore, is the only acceptable solution. "He heals the brokenhearted and binds up their wounds" (Ps. 147:3, ESV). Jesus will never desert us. He will never use us for personal gain. He won't give us excuses. He will only fill our empty spaces and mend our broken pieces. He makes us whole.

Emotionally, a relationship should only add on to your life. It should not be a substitute for anything and it definitely should not take away from you. You know what emotionally and spiritually healthy relationships look like? They look like two people who do not need to spend all of their time together. They look like people who can be happy even when they are apart. They look like people who have firm spiritual foundations of their own, but can push each other into deeper growth. They are people who pray and seek God together. They are people who live with Christ at the center of life rather than the other person. They are people who build one another up rather than pick at one another's faults, but they are also people who give correction and redirection where needed. *That* is healthy.

If what you want out of a relationship is someone to make you feel good, you've got the point of relationships all wrong. Stop looking for someone to hold your hand, to inflate your ego, to do nice things for you, and to take your side. God isn't looking to fill you up with another person. The truth is that if you're looking for that, you will find it, but it will be shallow, it will be fractured, and it will end in heartache. What God *is* looking to fill you with is His love, with His peace, and with His Spirit.

If you are in a place where you are determining what you want out of a relationship or what you expect out of a boyfriend/girlfriend, start with Jesus. You need to desire and seek after Jesus and, in turn, look for someone who is seeking Jesus as deeply and wholeheartedly as you are. Look for someone who will not pick at and exploit your flaws. Find someone who does not seek to take away from you—your life, your personality, your relationship with God—but seeks only to add on to your life. That may be hard to find. It may take a few tries to get it right, but I can promise you that it will be more worth it than you know.

Lesson 6: "[His] Work Is Never Finished and It's Never Past Due"

Glory be to God for that line from Cory Asbury's song "Water and Dust." Why? Because he fit this huge concept into a concise statement: God never finishes working on us, but when He finishes a piece of us, it is never late. Nothing He ever does is late or early. It simply comes to pass in the precise moment it should.

Often we think we know what is best for us. We try to dictate where and when God works in us and we try to decide when we think we have grown enough for the things we want. "God, you've taught me a ton and I've grown a ton [when you've barely grown at all], so now I should have the job/opportunity/relationship that I want." We don't have a clue what God has in store for us or when it will come to pass. God continues to work on us day in and day out because He loves us; because He wants what is best for us.

Here's the thing: God sees the entire picture. Have you ever tried to put together a puzzle without looking at the picture on the box? Puzzles can be hard enough to complete, but when you add this challenge, it adds on another dimension of difficulty to the process. When you can't see the picture, you often pick up pieces and place them in the completely wrong place. When we don't let God work on us in His way, it's like doing a puzzle without looking at the picture—it's doing things the hard way.

But God sees the whole picture. He knows how our lives will work out. He can see which pieces we need now and which pieces we will need later on. He knows which pieces fit together and which pieces just look like they should fit together. When we try to do it on our own, we make mistakes and the process takes longer. When God is in control, He gives us what we need precisely when we need it.

So while you may think you've got a handle on what does and does not need to change in your life, or whether you think you are done growing and changing into who God wants you to become (in general or for a relationship), you've got another thing coming. God never ceases to work on us. We will never be perfect, but He is always helping us come closer to perfection, reaching milestones exactly where and when we need to.

Chapter 8
Singleness as a Sacrifice

That is a scary title. It is scary for me to write it. Not many people happily give up the idea of being in a relationship. It is that deep desire for affection that we all have inside of us that makes it a hard concept to accept and carry out. Let's take a moment to clarify this phrase. "Singleness as a sacrifice" does not mean that you are giving up being single or sacrificing singleness. We are not talking about getting into a relationship just so that you are no longer single. That would probably be some of the worst advice I could ever give you about relationships. What I do mean is living a sacrificial lifestyle by being single.

Don't freak out. I can picture people getting frustrated or angry or sad because they think that I am saying that God is asking everyone to give up their desires for love and affection and live eternally single. I don't think that at all. If that is what God wanted, He would not have designed us with the ability to have romantic feelings and emotions. Are there some people who God does call to a lifetime of singleness and celibacy? Yes, there are, but they are not the majority. God knows what our desires are. He knows what our hearts long for, and while I truly believe He wants to give us those desires, I also believe that sometimes He calls us to something beyond those desires.

When we talk about singleness as a sacrifice, we are really talking about obedience. In fact, sacrifice and obedience go hand in hand in many areas of life. When God calls you into the ministry, being obedient may require you to sacrifice what you thought your future would be like. When God asks you to sacrifice something you love, He may be trying to teach you to be obedient. Obedience is not always an easy thing. It is easy to obey rules and requests when they make you feel good or they make your life better. It is difficult to obey rules and requests when they cost you something.

We are selfish beings, so when God asks us to give up something that we value and love, obedience can be a source of inner conflict. Have you ever felt that conflict before? I don't mean just with relationships; I mean in life. Have you ever had that feeling where you know that God is asking you to do something—to sacrifice something—but the personal cost just seems to be too great? Most often I have found that the thing that obedience costs us is our comfort. "God, I would pray for that person, but it's just out of my comfort zone." "But, God, what if I say the wrong thing and get embarrassed?"

That's personal cost? How petty and insignificant my comfort seems to be when I consider things that have real personal cost. Things like dying for people who do not know you, do not care about you, and do not want your sacrifice, like dying for crimes you never committed. Yes, I am talking about Jesus. How can I compare my discomfort and possible embarrassment with Christ's sacrifice on the cross? How can I feel like God is asking too much of me when He sent His own son to die for me? How can I question obeying the Holy Spirit when Christ made a way for me to escape my sin? How can I weigh my temporary disappointment against the eternal joy that I have been given? I shouldn't, but sometimes I do.

Jesus wasn't the only person in the Bible who experienced great personal sacrifice. How about we talk about someone who wasn't a part of the trinity? Let's talk about Abraham. Abraham made plenty of sacrifices in his life, just as we all do, but I would argue that one of the greatest, faith-building sacrifices that Abraham ever made was to literally sacrifice his own son.

If you are new to this Christianity thing and you're not familiar with the story, you *did* read that correctly. God asked Abraham to literally sacrifice his son. Let's backtrack a little because this story is important for where I'm headed in this chapter and I want to make sure that you are following. Abraham and God have gone through a lot together. There have been instances of obedience, trust, and faith, and there have been mistakes, times of stubbornness, and times of delayed obedience (all on Abraham's part). Overall, though, God sees Abraham as a faithful and trusted servant, and God promises Abraham that he will have descendants as numerous as the stars in the sky (Gen. 15). When Abraham and his wife are well past the age that people should or are physically able to have children, they have a son and name him Isaac (Gen. 21).

Not only is it a miracle that Isaac is born to people of such advanced age, but his birth was also the beginning of the fulfillment of the covenant that God made with Abraham. Then God asked Abraham to do what any parent today would consider unthinkable. He asked Abraham to take his son—his promised son, his son that was a miracle, his son that was the fulfillment of a covenant with God—and lay him down on an altar to sacrifice him. Talk about inner conflict; talk about personal sacrifice. We don't get to read about how Abraham felt about this test from God. The Bible simply tells us that God told him to offer Isaac as a sacrifice, and that Abraham rose, prepared, and left to do it, but we can imagine how he may have felt. It is probably pretty safe to say that he was a bit confused by the situation. I am sure he did not understand the request, but Abraham knew who God was. He knew that God was sovereign, that He was all-powerful, and that He would keep His promises. So, in what I would consider one of the greatest acts of faith *ever*, Abraham saddled his donkey and set off to offer his son as a burnt offering to God.

Have you ever been willing to go to such lengths to please God? I honestly don't think I have been or would have been that faithful to Him, but He is always faithful to us. He was as faithful to Abraham as Abraham was to Him. If you continue to read Genesis 22, you will see a number of things happen. On approaching the mountain, Isaac asks his father what they will be sacrificing since they have not brought an animal with them, and Abraham tells him that God will provide a sacrifice. That is faith. That is trust. When they get to the place where the sacrifice will happen, they build the altar. Abraham binds up his son—his promised son, his miracle son, his covenant son—and places him on the altar.

> Then he reached out his hand and took the knife to slay his son. But the angel of the Lord called out to him from heaven, "Abraham! Abraham!" "Here I am," he replied. "Do not lay a hand on the boy," he said. "Do not do anything to him. Now I know that you fear God, because you have not withheld from me your son, your only son." Abraham looked up and there in a thicket he saw a ram caught by its horns. He went over and took the ram and sacrificed it as a burnt offering instead of his son. (Gen. 22:10–13, NIV)

Abraham withheld nothing from God, not even his son. There is a reason why he is referred to as a "giant of the faith." Whether he believed God would spare him the sacrifice, raise his son from the dead, or provide him with another son, Abraham knew that God would be faithful to him. He knew that God would fulfill the promises He made.

It was this story of sacrifice that led me to living a lifestyle of singleness as a sacrifice in a season of waiting for the right person. I felt alone and forgotten. I felt insecure. I felt like I had been deprived of something. God had promised me that he would give me a husband someday, so I believed I deserved to have that person in my life now. You see, I thought I had given control over to God, and sometimes I really did give it to him for a day or two at a time, but I would invariably take back the control and fall back into the simultaneous feelings of sadness and entitlement. We all talk about how we want Christ to be the center of our lives and of our relationships, but we are not obedient, we hold tight to control, and we refuse to sacrifice portions of our lives.

I don't know if you have figured this out yet or not, but the Holy Spirit's moving in your life is exponentially more powerful and affective when you break down all of the walls that you have built up in your heart and embrace it. Listen carefully, the Holy Spirit still moves and works whether or not you give all of yourself to it, but its manifestation in someone with a hardened heart is drastically different from its manifestation in someone with a totally surrendered heart. For a lot of us, that fullness of the Spirit looks like us surrendering control, and for some of us it is more specifically surrendering control of our relationships.

The thought of being single for the rest of my life is something that scared and worried me for many years. When you constantly see people in love—whether in real life, on television, or in books—it makes sense to desire that in your own life. Being single has this appearance of sadness and loneliness, and if you allow it to be that way, it will be. However, it does not have to be. Singleness is what you make of it.

When I suggest that God may be calling you to a life/season of singleness, what I am suggesting is that God may be trying to weed out things that you value above Him. He may be helping you evaluate how much faith and trust you place in Him versus in other people. When it comes to some matters in life, specifically matters of the heart, Christians have a habit of living in a paradox where they know that God is always faithful, yet they act like the only person they can trust is themselves.

Abraham couldn't see the outcome of his situation, but he knew that God is always faithful. He had seen it before, he had experienced it before, and he lived a lifestyle that reflected his belief in God's faithfulness. I know what it is like to be single and be surrounded by people who are happily in relationships. All of my core friends from college were engaged, married, and having children before I had found another serious relationship. That can be discouraging, and when I ask you to consider living single as a sacrifice for a period of time, it can be scary. For a period of time in my life, God has placed me in this season of being single in a sacrificial way.

When God asks us to do things, He often doesn't give us a timeline or an end date. That is where He is looking for faith. That is where He is looking for obedience.

We begin to exercise faith in sacrifice when we are obedient outside of knowing the future and outside of knowing the outcome.

Abraham couldn't see the outcome—God gave him a task and waited for him to be obedient in that instance before revealing more of the plan to him. It may not be God's plan to keep you single forever, but sacrificing your control and your desires might be a test of loyalty, a test of surrender. God wants all of you, not just what you are willing to part with.

Abraham was able to be faithful and obedient to God because he knew and had experienced how faithful God is. If Abraham served a god that was selfish, untrustworthy, and didn't keep his word, he probably would not have had the courage to follow through with what was asked of him, nor would he have had the reason to. I don't know about you, but I serve the God of the Bible. The same unchanging, steadfast, and loving God that delivered nations from captivity. The same God that shut the mouths of lions and caused walls to come tumbling down with the mere sound of voices. The same God who allowed His son to take my place in death. And yes, the very same God who asked Abraham to sacrifice his son, but provided an animal in his place.

That is a faithful God. We can talk all about having faith and trusting God's plan, but the Bible tells us that faith without works is dead (James 2:17). It would have been easy for Abraham to tell God that he *would* be faithful *if* God asked him to sacrifice his son. Words are cheap. Most of the time words don't cost us a thing. Actions, however, come at a higher price. When Abraham made preparations, set out, and began carrying out the task that God set before him, that is when God truly saw how much faith Abraham had.

When God asked me to live a lifestyle of singleness as a sacrifice, it was something that I struggled with initially. In my head I told God about how I had been living sacrificially single for the last four years, but in my heart I knew that there was nothing sacrificial about it. They were four years that were at many times defined by the search for someone to spend my life with. In fact, when God asked this of me, I was many months deep into a friendship where I was hoping, praying, and waiting for it to turn into more. There was no sacrifice up to that point. I had given up nothing to be single. It was simply an unwanted but prolonged season of singleness.

To willingly step into or embrace a season of singleness, it takes a lot of faith. If God is asking you to be single in a sacrificial way, it is going to require sacrifice. Kind of a "duh" statement, right? For me, that meant distancing myself from that person who I wanted a relationship with. It meant taking a step back and refocusing my thoughts and conversations: turning them away from him and turning them toward God. It meant denying myself. Embracing the season of singleness may mean other kinds of sacrifice for you. It could be that you have to stop looking around every corner for the person you want to marry. It could mean pursuing something that God called you to that requires you to be alone.

Whatever the sacrifice is, it will require faith. I can't tell you what the sacrifice is or how to go about it. That is between you and God. What I can tell you is that there is always room for improvement when it comes to our walk with God. I know for a fact that up to this point I have never exercised the amount of faith that Abraham did. I also know for a fact that God is asking me to have that type of radical faith. How can I trust God and have faith in His huge plans for my life when I can't trust Him with something smaller? Something smaller like remaining single when He asks me to.

Now is the time to put your money where your mouth is. Now is the time to make your actions match your words. Find yourself an altar, or make yourself an altar. Find a place where you can get on your knees. I'm serious. Make a big deal out of it. Do the physical motions because it will make a difference. Offer your singleness to God. Don't offer it as something to be burned up and done away with, but offer it as something to be used and repurposed for His will and His glory. We underestimate the power of physical posture in our spiritual lives. Sure, we can pray or worship from any physical place, but the act of getting on one's knees or of jumping and dancing in His presence can make such a huge difference.

Like I said before, living single as a sacrifice is not a life sentence. It is an exercise of trust, of faith, of obedience, and of growth. If you've never asked God what He desires for your relationships, it is time to start. If you have never given God the control of your relationships, now is the time. Maybe this is your wake-up call. Maybe this is God telling you that you are allowing other things to come between His relationship with you. Maybe being single is just the thing you need to step into the life and the calling that God has for you.

Chapter 9
Dating 102 (Part 1)

Welcome, and thank you for enrolling in Dating 102. The aim of this course is to re-teach individuals what it means to date someone and how dating should look in a Christian relationship. It is also the aim of this course to redirect some of what you've previously learned, and help young people construct healthier and more successful views and practices when it comes to dating.

———

Okay, so this isn't actually going to be a formal course on how to/not to go about dating, but it may be helpful to get yourself into a learning mindset for what we are going to talk about. When I say a "learning mindset," I definitely do not mean the mindset you had in high school where you dazed off, fell asleep, and only committed things to your short-term memory. I mean an actual learning mindset where you consciously make the decision to focus on what is being said and figure out how to apply it in life. Ready?

We've talked a little bit about what ideas the church—whether directly or indirectly—puts out there about dating and relationships. But for the sake of a comprehensive discussion, let's review. When I was growing up in the church, I got the following ideas about how to date:

1. The other person needs to be (or call themselves) a Christian.
2. You need to become best friends before you date.
3. Going on one date means you're in a full-blown relationship.

Now, I will be the first to admit that not all of these things are wrong, not all of them are entirely bad, and that some of them have led to many healthy relationships/marriages. I will also be the first to tell you that those pathways to marriage that are more widely celebrated or recognizable in the church are not the only ways to get there. There is no perfect formula or timeline of life for you to use to experience a healthy and God-centered relationship that turns into a healthy and God-centered marriage. There are, however, principles that you can live by to save you some heartache and save you from some of those relationships you may label as mistakes in the future.

In chapter 4 I talked about your dating requirements and how the seemingly simple question of whether or not someone is a Christian is actually much deeper than we tend to think it is when we are in middle and high school. I looked at the label of Christian as a stamp of approval when it came to dating. If he said he was a Christian, he was dateable. If he didn't say he was a Christian, I had to get him to church, get him saved, and *then* he would be dateable. I am a little ashamed to admit that I did at one point bring someone I was interested in to youth group because I knew I couldn't date him if he didn't love Jesus (we call that missionary dating). As an adolescent, I never took in to account levels of spiritual maturity or theological alignment when I considered people to date. And why would I? It is not often that a fourteen- or fifteen-year-old has a long-term relationship, let alone one long enough to lead to a marriage. Even if young people in the church are not explicitly looking for or finding relationships that are headed toward marriage, these are important ideas to begin making them aware of when they begin going on dates and getting into relationships because it helps them to be mindful and observant of how the people they are interested act and speak.

Those conversations are extremely important for two people who are getting into a relationship to have *before* getting into a commitment. No one wants to waste their time with someone they could not see a future with. So how do you have those conversations before getting into a relationship? Hopefully, you're not texting about it. Hopefully, if you're really interested in a person you are talking to them face-to-face about important things of this nature. I have a revolutionary idea for you on how and when to have these conversations. You go on something called a date. A date can be just the two of you or it can be in a group setting. It is an opportunity for you to get together with a person outside of your typical interactions in a setting where you are able to learn more about the person and what is important to them.

A date is not a commitment. A date does not make a relationship. First dates are supposed to be a time where you admit to shared interest or attraction, and you figure out whether someone is worth committing to. No promises, no guarantees, minimal pain. That is the situation in which the question "is he/she a Christian" *can* be a requirement. I wouldn't consider dating someone who doesn't even claim to be a Christian, and neither should you. But, for those who do call themselves Christ-followers, a date or two is where you can find out how committed to Christ they are and if they check all of the boxes (spiritual, theological, and otherwise) on your "must have" dating list.

If they still live up to what you're looking for after a few dates, it's probably time to have a conversation about dating exclusively. If they are not living up to what you're looking for, the good news is that you never committed to them and there should not be much, if any, attachment to make it painful. It's not a breakup, because it was never a relationship to begin with. Here's the catch though: you can't disappear, you have to be an adult and have a conversation with them about what/why it's not working. If you just cut them out of your life with no explanation, there will be pain and confusion and bitterness on their end.

Something that I heard all of the time growing up is that you need to become best friends with the person you like before you ever date them. This attitude is perpetuated based off the fact that married people always say that they are married to their best friend. Sure, that is sweet, and I aim to be best friends with the person I marry, but that is in no way, shape, or form a required precursor to a successful relationship. When you like a person, it is normal to want to be around them and spend time with them, but I know that I personally fell into a continuous trap where I thought that becoming best friends with the person I liked would end in him falling in love with me in some magical Hallmark way.

Life doesn't really work the way that it does on television, and real love stories usually happen in less cinematic ways. If there is someone that you are starting to have feelings for that you also see as someone who could be a valuable friend to you, you're better off trying to date first (or at least discussing your feelings) and then being friends if it doesn't work out. The less attachment there is, the easier it is to get over and maintain a friendship. This is quite contrary to that statement that you're constantly told as a young person: date your best friend. What I'm suggesting is this: date someone you are *not* best friends with.

When you build a friendship based off the hope that the other person will fall for you someday, there are a number of scenarios that can play out. You could be one of the lucky few whose best friend falls in love with them in the end. You could also be lucky in the sense that when your real feelings do come out and they are not reciprocated, your friendship does not suffer. However, there are more likely and more common outcomes to this situation such as suppressed feelings, lowered self-esteem, and fractured friendships.

The sad reality of life is that the majority of the population does not react well when they find out that someone has feelings for them that they can't or don't return. That fear leaves many people stuck in silence, counting the days until the other person feels the same way or until they themselves get over those feelings. It's a recipe for disaster. Talk about your feelings in the beginning and get the closure you need to move on.

Another important thing to express when it comes to (not) dating your best friend is this: the only people who become instant best friends when they meet are kindergarteners. It is unrealistic to expect two people to meet for the first time and interact as though they were already best friends. The comfort, knowledge, laughs, and closeness are not things that are expected initially. They are things that grow between two people. If that is how we see friendships, why is that not how we see relationships?

We have to stop pushing this idea that you need to know everything about a person before a relationship because part of being in a relationship is the process of learning everything about the person you care about. Part of being in a relationship is that process of becoming best friends. That process of becoming best friends in the midst of a relationship is often part of what lets you know that they are the right person for you to be with.

If you do find the strength to express your feelings to someone and find yourself going on a date, there are a few things you should know. First of all, don't spill all of your secrets. If you spill all of your deepest secrets, desires, and failures to someone on the first date—or even in the first few dates—you're probably going to get burned. Why? Because you are trusting them with pieces of your heart that they have not earned yet. What happens if they move on or if they get upset with you? They have those secrets that they didn't earn to use against you at their will. On more than one occasion, I've seen people use someone's testimony and the sins that they have been delivered from as a weapon against them when things go wrong. You need to make sure that the people you are trusting with your heart are worthy of that trust. That's why you don't spill it all on date number one or two or three. That is a part of building the relationship, and a date or two does not equal a relationship.

I'm going to say that again because it is incredibly important for you to understand that *a date or two does not equal a relationship*. This is a crazy-huge trap that crazy-huge numbers of people fall into. When a guy asks a girl on a date, that does not make him her boyfriend. When a girl agrees to go on a date with a guy, that does not make her his girlfriend. The purpose of the first few dates with a person is to decide *if* you want a relationship with them. I think that one of the few things I really did right in my high school/college long-term relationship is that I did not let the guy I dated a few times just start calling me his girlfriend. We had been texting for a long time and had been on multiple dates, but I told him that it was not a relationship and I was not his girlfriend until he actually asked. Why? Because I felt he owed me the DTR (defining the relationship) talk, and because I wanted him to understand that he couldn't just assume things about our relationship, but that he had to talk to me instead.

I am proud of my seventeen-year-old self for that decision, but it is one that I learned to make because I operated in the total opposite way in a previous relationship. When I was a sophomore in high school I had my first boyfriend (you know, besides the ones I had as a toddler). Except we never went on a date, and it only lasted for two weeks. I liked him, he liked me, we told everyone we were in a relationship, and now I am stuck with him labeled as my "first boyfriend." All that simply because I didn't understand that (a) someone does not have to be your boyfriend *before* you go on a date, (b) going on a date does not equal a relationship, and (c) dating someone helps you to figure out if you want a relationship.

If I had gone on a date with this boy, I would have discovered that I did not truly have feelings for him, but that I liked the attention I was getting from him. If I had just gone on a date, I could have had a different first boyfriend. If I had gone on a date, I could have spared us both some awkwardness/pain. If I had gone on a date, we wouldn't have had to deal with quite so many people's input about our relationship/breakup. If I had just gone on a date, things would have been far, far simpler.

I told you both of those stories to reiterate that statement that a date or two does not equal a relationship. Do I sound like a broken record now? When I was in high school, my youth pastor told us that "anything worth remembering is worth repeating" (Joel Dahlstrom). So, I will repeat it as many times as it takes to let it get engraved in your mind, because if young people in the church begin to understand that concept and embrace it, we might find that dates aren't so scary, that new relationships aren't too difficult, and that hearts get broken less often.

The process of beginning to date a person *can* be a scary one, and when you are a young person, relationships feel like they have the power to make or break you. And they do, but only if you let them. However old you are, however many relationships you have had, the most important thing for you to make sure you do is make Christ the center of all of it. If Christ is at the center, even on simple, non-committal dates, it is not only going to improve the situation, but it will also improve you.

I'd like to make the point that you should be involving God *before* you commit to a relationship with someone. If you have a habit of getting into a relationship and *then* asking God what He thinks, you're doing things backward. Use the Spirit of God to help you discern who to give your time to. I'll tell you right now that it is not a fun conversation to have with your new boyfriend or girlfriend when you have to tell them you need to break up with them because you weren't supposed to be in a relationship in the first place and you were just ignoring what God was telling you.

If we begin to change the dialogue and attitudes about dating within the church, we will begin to see change in our young people. If we cut out that incessant need for immediate commitment, I truly believe that we will see less heartache. Why? Because heartache comes from attachment, and we attach to people far too quickly. While there may be many reasons for this disease of rapid affection, I would suggest that the deepest underlying one is that we are not attached to Christ—we do not have enough affection for Christ. When you don't have a deep connection with something, it is easy for other things to come along and steal your attention. If you aren't already attached to the love of God, if you don't already find your strength and comfort in Him, it is so easy to allow a person (even one you barely know) to become that strength and comfort. Don't trap yourself in a relationship with someone because you became attached to them too quickly instead of being attached to Christ.

───

So what have we learned about dating so far? 1. Use your first few dates with someone to figure out how committed to Christ he or she is and to figure out if he or she is even a good fit for you. 2. You do *not* need to be best friends with someone to date them. In fact, that often makes things harder if they don't work out. 3. *Dates do not equal a relationship!* (I think you're starting to get that concept now.) And, even in these early stages of dating, 4. Love Jesus before you try to love someone else.

Chapter 10
Dating 102 (Part 2)

Part 2! In this section of Dating 102, we are going to talk a little bit about what we see/learn from church once Christians are in committed relationships. "But wait! This is a book about being single. Why are you talking about dating?" Well, my dear friends, until you've got a ring on your finger, you're single. So, we are going to talk about what your relationships should look like. But first, let's get a general outline of how things have gone to get you to this place.

> Step 1: You and the person that you like develop some level of attraction to each other.
> Step 2: One person asks the other out on a date to get to know each other better.
> Step 3: The two of you proceed to go on a date, have fun, and decide to go on another date.
> (Alternate Step 3: You go on a date and decide that you would be better off as just friends.)
> Step 4: The two of you go on a few more dates and continue to get to know each other/enjoy your time together.
> Step 5: You feel like you want to commit to the other person so you have the DTR—define the relationship—talk and you become boyfriend and girlfriend.

And that brings us to where we are now. You are in a relationship, and I pray that you have been consulting Jesus through this whole process. But, what have you heard about Christian relationships? What have you observed through the church's attitudes toward relationships? These are the ideas I got as a teen and throughout college about healthy relationships:

1. No sex and no physical activity that will lead you to sex.
2. Most Christians marry the first person they have a serious relationship with.
3. Most Christians get married young and fast.

Again, not necessarily all wrong and not necessarily all bad. Let's take a look at that first one. It is very clear in the Bible that you should not be having sex outside of marriage, but the range of what Christians believe is acceptable to do physically up to that point is quite varied. Some of what people believe comes from the Bible, and some of it has to do with their own scruples—or their own convictions. This is because we all have different levels of self-control, and because the Holy Spirit convicts us differently based off what He knows we can and cannot handle in terms of temptation.

You will find Christians with beliefs that range from no kissing until your wedding day all the way to anything but actual sex is acceptable. You will even find single Christians who maintain a sexually active lifestyle with no convictions about it. In fact, I heard a statistic recently that 80 percent of evangelical young adults are having sex before they are married.[1] I'm not sure how accurate that is, but even the possibility of the numbers being that high is scary.

There is something that has been lost in translation for those people. There is something about God's word that is not clicking for them. Perhaps initially there was conviction, but the thing with sin is that the more you give in to it, the less it weighs on your heart. This is because you are allowing the enemy to take root in you and allowing him to use your disobedience to distance you from God and make you deaf to the correction of His Spirit. If you find yourself in that situation, where you have given in to sexual temptation and contin-

---

[1] Tavera, Bianca, and Lightworkers. "Alarming Report: 80% of Unmarried Evangelical Young Adults Are Having Sex." Charisma News, 25 July 2019, 7:00, www.charismanews.com/culture/77317-alarming-report-80-of-unmarried-evangelical-young-adults-are-having-sex.

ually live in that sin, call upon God's name. He is Jehovah-Mephalti, the Lord my deliverer, and if you believe it, He is powerful enough to deliver you from whatever sin you have found yourself entangled in.

If you are not in that situation, that means you find yourself somewhere on the spectrum between barely abstinent and barely making eye contact with someone of the opposite sex. The Bible tells us over and over to flee from sexual immorality, or sexual sin. In fact, we are even told that thinking sexual or lustful thoughts about someone who is not your spouse is a sin (Matt. 5:28). So there is a big check mark next to number one on the list: no sex. We're going to get really honest here for a second. When I say no sex, I don't just mean in a traditional sense. I am telling you to run from any situation where clothes come off or where hands/mouths end up where they have no business. Why? Because that kind of intimacy is what leaves people devastated when relationships do not work out. Because that kind of intimacy is only meant for the person that you have committed yourself to for the rest of your life through marriage.

In Song of Solomon, Solomon's beloved says, "Do not arouse or awaken love until it so desires" (8:4b, NIV). She speaks this to her friends with the warning that "love is as strong as death," that "it burns like a blazing fire" (v.6). "Many waters cannot quench love; rivers cannot sweep it away" (v.7). When you allow yourself into situations that awaken love prematurely, you are inviting chaos into your life. A fire that cannot be quenched brings death and destruction, just as intimacy and passion outside of a marriage can.[2] This is why I caution you against any situation that may be a temptation for you and your significant other. This is why you set up boundaries. This is why you have other people to help keep you accountable in your relationship.

If you read God's word, there is no argument that those sexual acts should not be occurring outside of marriage, but there are other, smaller acts in a relationship that show love and affection that are

---

[2] Marsteller, Paula. "Arousing and Awakening Love… Some Other Day!" *Lies Young Women Believe*, 26 May 2011, liesyoungwomenbelieve.com/arousing-and-awakening-love-some-other-day/.

not by definition sinful, but that some people still stay away from. Things like holding hands, kissing, sitting close together, and spending time alone together, to name a few. I wouldn't say that any of those things are wrong in a general sense, but there are people who they are wrong for.

There are a lot of things in life that have the ability to lead you astray. These are areas in which you need to listen hard to what the Spirit of God is telling you. If you have a strong sense of conviction about those things happening before you are married, then stay away from them. There is nothing wrong with that, and you shouldn't let other people make you feel wrong about doing what God has asked of you. That is another thing that we as a church need to work on. We often question people when they feel convictions that we do not, but we don't know their past. We don't know their weaknesses or their struggles. We don't know what might be too much of a temptation for them, so we have no right to judge or make fun of what they feel convicted about.

"Therefore let us not pass judgment on one another any longer, but rather decide never to put a stumbling block or hindrance in the way of a brother" (Rom. 14:13, ESV).

Wherever you find yourself on that spectrum of what is and is not acceptable in a relationship, you *must* make sure of two things:

1. You need to live a pure and holy life as laid out for you in God's word. You need to run from anything that the Bible would deem immoral.
2. You need to listen to the Spirit. Accept His convictions and do not allow people to make you feel ashamed for doing what God has asked of you.

The next thing that I noticed about Christian relationships is that a lot of Christians marry the first person they ever have a real relationship with. There's nothing wrong with that. In fact, I would consider those people lucky. They're lucky to have found the right person on the first try. They're lucky to have never had to start over from scratch after a relationship has ended. We aren't all that lucky.

Or at least, we aren't all lucky in that sense. I know I'm not lucky in that sense, but I also know that it doesn't mean that when I do get married it won't be successful.

I included this point in this chapter (at the risk of repeating myself) because I don't want to keep seeing people trapped in relationships or staying with their "first love" out of fear of starting over or for the sake of calling him or her the first. When you find the right person to be with, other "loves" you have had in the past won't compare. When you find the right person to be with, you will feel like the lucky one. The important thing for you to remember when you look around and see people like my best friend who married the boy she started dating as a sophomore in high school, is that your story doesn't have to look like someone else's story. And, while the "we met at Christian camp at sixteen and got married after college" story is a valid one (that I have heard a surprising number of times), it is not the formula for happiness.

The danger of getting into the mindset that marrying the first person you date defines success is that in the end it will result in failure for a number of reasons. First, you're staying in the relationship for the wrong reason. Second, you're not thinking long term (like twenty or thirty years into a marriage you convinced yourself you should have). Third, you're ignoring those nagging feelings that are most likely coming from the Holy Spirit trying to push you in the right direction. You know what the single, most important thing is when it comes to relationships? Tuning out what the world says to you and expects of you and tuning in to what God says to you and expects of you.

I don't know how many times I can say that God does not want you to suffer or to feel defeated. His desire is to give you the things that you desire. The catch is this: He knows how to better fulfill and meet those desires than we do. In Mark Batterson's book *The Circle Maker*, he talks about looking for office space that his church not only wanted but truly was in need of. They found a place, it was perfect, and it fell through. Then the unthinkable happened. They found a new place, it was even better than the first one, and it fell through again. They felt like God was opposing them, but then something truly God ordained occurred. They were blessed with a building that was somehow better than the two they had missed out on.

Not only did God provide for their current needs and desires, but he provided them with more than they expected, more than they asked for, and with a building that would be advantageous to them when their next dream came along. If God answered their prayers initially, or if they were stubborn and tried to do things on their own, things would not have worked out the way they did. If God just gave them what they thought they needed or wanted at the time, "He would have given [them] second or third best" (*The Circle Maker*, page 126).

Maybe God doesn't want you to have second or third best in a marriage. Maybe God wants you to have His first choice. But really, there are no "maybes" about it. God does want you to have His first choice for a husband or wife, but if you give in to the idea that things will be more magical because you married your first love, you're settling for second or third best. If you convince yourself that it will be too hard to start over now, you're settling for second or third best.

The other thing that I gleaned from my time as a youth and as a college student is that Christians get married young, fast, or both. This, once again, is not something that is wrong for everyone, but it is *definitely* not something that is right for everyone. And, above that, it is not something that should have ever become so normalized in the church that we started to make young people feel like they missed a milestone, missed their chance, or failed in some way.

Why? Because while our twenty-somethings are the future of the church, they are also the present church, and if a church is filled with people who either feel defeated and inadequate or make other people feel defeated and inadequate, it is not going to do any good for the kingdom of God. Sure, that sounds extreme, but that is what church can become, and the church is not supposed to be a place of defeat. Instead, the church should be a place of victory.

How do we bring the church to a place where young people can be confident whether they are in a relationship or not? We shut down the narrative that celebrates the twenty-two-year-olds that are married and questions the twenty-four-year-olds that are single. The problem here isn't that some Christians get married during college or right out of college. The problem here is that every single time I see someone I know from a Christian setting who I haven't seen in a while, one of the first things they ask me is if I am dating somebody—that is a question that you need to earn the right to ask, or at the very least work up to. The problem is when people older than myself try to project their "I met *my* husband in college" experience on to my life and see that it doesn't measure up—that is how the church breeds feelings of failure and insecurity.

If those types of experiences resonate with you, you're not alone. But here is the thing: you can't hang around and ignore those things when you hear them anymore. That is why this has become such a problem. What needs to happen is that those of us that understand this concept need to speak up. I am all for being respectful to people in authority over you or people who are older than you, but what I am not for is holding my tongue while those people make me feel like I have failed when I have simply been walking along the path that God has set out for me.

And let me tell you this:

Comparison either breeds pride or steals joy. Neither of those things have a place in the Kingdom of God.

I don't want to be in a church that is not victorious. I don't want to be in a church that only validates young people (especially young women) once there's a ring on their finger. I don't want to be part of a church that only wants married couples to be a part of their leadership/ministry. I want to be a part of a church that empowers its young people to win spiritual ground without thinking about their relationship status. I want to be a part of a church where people stop expecting my life to look like their own and begin to celebrate the journey God has given me to His call and His promises. A church like that is one well on its way to becoming unstoppable.

The bottom line is that many Christians do get married young. Sometimes for the right reasons and sometimes for the wrong ones. Many Christians get married after only dating for a short time. Again, sometimes for the right reasons and sometimes for the wrong reasons. Both of those things are okay if they are in God's plan. You know what else is okay if it is in God's plan? Taking your time in a relationship before committing to marriage; not settling for marrying someone that may be God's second or third choice for you; enjoying and embracing the time God has given you to be single.

Lesson 7: Dating Ain't Married; Engaged Ain't Married

There are a couple of different points that I would like to make based off of that statement.

1. I don't care how long you've been together. If you're not married, don't do married things.
2. I don't care how long you've been together. If you're not married, you can break up.

A lot of young people get to a point in their relationship where they have been together for so long that they think the standards of purity no longer apply to them. They may say, "Oh, we are going to get married someday anyway..." This often happens to engaged couples as well who obviously have decided to commit to each other in marriage and decide that there's no point in waiting to act like they're married.

Well, well, well, if you direct your attention to point number two, you will notice that if you aren't married, you can still break up. I happen to know multiple different people who have had broken engagements, never mind all of the people who were dating and expected to marry their significant other, but broke up in the end (myself included). There is no such thing as "as good as married." You're married, or you're not, and there isn't much more to say on that matter.

So, if you get into a relationship and you find yourself justifying actions by saying you'll get married eventually, *or* if you find yourself thinking that you've put so much time and effort into the relationship already that you have to get married, you're wrong. Dating ain't married, and engaged ain't married. Don't compromise and definitely don't settle.

Chapter 11
Be Someone Worth Dating

This is a tough topic to talk about because a lot of what I'm going to say can easily be misinterpreted and turned into things that are not intended. You're going to have to bear with me as we dive into this idea of being someone that is "worth it" to date. I want to make three things clear off the bat:

1. You do not need to—nor should you—change the essence of who you are to become "dateable."
2. You do not need to alter your appearance to *be* beautiful.
3. Faking or forcing change to gain a relationship will be disastrous.

God has created you as a unique individual. He made you with talents, interests, strengths, and weaknesses that, when combined, make you one of a kind. Not much of this world is one of a kind anymore. Everything seems to be mass produced and mass marketed. Things that are mass produced carry less value because they become common. Uncommon things are the things that intrigue people. People will spend exorbitant amounts of money on one-of-a-kind art, cars, clothes, etc., but the reason they have so much value is that they are unique.

Do you see where I am headed here? When you try to change who you are to become like someone else, or to become someone who you think other people want you to be, you begin to devalue and alter the one-of-a-kind person that God created you to be. I don't know about you, but I think it's exhausting (and a little bit irritating) to look around and see cookie-cutter individuals who dress the same, buy the same things, and have the same interests.

Something that I have learned over the years is that inward beauty informs and reflects outward beauty. I know that sounds like a line we tell to people who don't consider themselves attractive, but it really is the truth. It doesn't matter how pretty or handsome you are; if you're ugly on the inside, it reflects on the outside. The same is true the opposite way. Perhaps you don't feel like you meet the world's standard of beauty, but you have a beautiful heart. That type of beauty is not one you're likely to notice when you look at yourself in the mirror, but it is one that other people see when they look at you. It is a beauty that emanates from you when people see you and speak to you.

When I first met the boy I dated in college, it wasn't his appearance that attracted me to him but his personality. As I began to find and see the pieces of his heart that were attractive to me, it reflected outwardly. You see, being someone that it is worth it to pursue and worth it to date has nothing to do with what you look like and everything to do with who you are. Short-lived relationships that were based off physical attraction tend to feel like mistakes. Relationships that were based on more—that were based on knowing who a person is—still hurt when they end, but typically leave you with the feeling that you somehow grew because of them.

This idea of inner beauty is biblical too. 1 Peter 3:3–4, ESV says, "Do not let your adorning be external—the braiding of hair and the putting on of gold jewelry, or the clothing you wear—but let your adorning be the hidden person of the heart with the imperishable beauty of a gentle and quiet spirit, which in God's sight is precious." That hidden beauty inside of you is what is pleasing to God. He doesn't really care what clothes you have on, what expensive sneakers you wear, or how you do your makeup today because those things don't make you more beautiful to Him. Those are silly human things. When God measures beauty, He weighs your heart and He looks at your spirit.

What does it look like to become someone who is a worthy dating option? It has to do with becoming physically healthy, emotionally healthy, and spiritually healthy. When I say physically healthy, I'm not telling you to try to fit into any type of standard you or the world holds "healthy" (or attractive) to. I am telling you to take care of yourself. Take care of the body God has given you. Stop treating it poorly and feeding it poorly, because taking care of yourself is a way of honoring God.

Taking care of yourself has personal benefits too. When you take care of your body, it works better. You'll have more energy and feel better all around when you start to eat, sleep, and exercise the way you should. There is also something attractive about a people who take care of themselves. Not just in any physical improvements that come with the healthy choices but also in the attitude that comes with being healthy.

In relationships there are times when you take care of each other, but you should not have to constantly worry about the other person's health and well-being because they are unconcerned with it themselves. A boyfriend, girlfriend, or spouse isn't supposed to come into your life and take care of you like a parent does with an infant. If you present yourself in that manner, people aren't going to want to be with you. Maybe that's harsh, but it's the truth. It can be hard enough taking care of yourself, never mind having to take care of another grown adult.

Becoming physically healthy is only the first step here. Emotional health is also an important part of being ready for a relationship. We all come with baggage. We all come with past hurts, failures, and disappointments. There are broken and mending pieces inside each and every one of us. The key to being emotionally healthy lies within how you react to and move forward from those things.

If I held on to all of my broken pieces, I would be an emotional wreck—the kind that is so bad you just can't seem to look away. I would be a mixed up mess of trust issues, heartache, self-pity, anger, and resentment, but (for the most part) I am none of those things. You see, God has this incredible ability to heal us of pain and hurt that seems never-ending. He's not going to do it without your permission though. He's not going to force healing on you if you are desiring to wallow in your brokenness. That healing is a gift that you can choose to accept or deny. (I'd choose to accept it if I were you. It really changes things.)

I am not the broken person I was or could be, and all the glory goes to God for that. All that baggage I could have held on to is far too much to bring into a relationship. It's also not fair to the other person to bring all kinds of unresolved things like that into a relationship. This is why it is so important to be in an emotionally healthy place beforehand. Emotional health is something that you have to constantly evaluate. A lot of times people think they have dealt with hurts from their past only to discover once they are in a relationship that they weren't as dealt-with as they thought. If you get yourself into the habit of asking God what you need to work on, let go of, and allow Him to heal in you, those broken pieces will be uncovered and begin to mend.

Emotional health isn't about having it all together. It's about being able to identify where your emotions may be clouded and working toward clearing away those clouds with God's help.

The most important thing when it comes to being "dateable" is your spiritual health. I will tell you, as a woman of God who is watching for that person to spend her life with, there are few things as attractive as a man who loves the Lord and seeks after Him whole-heartedly. I will also tell you that, as a woman of God, His Spirit makes it easy to discern who is seeking God for his own benefit and who is seeking God for *my* benefit. It is an important thing to know too, because it is a huge indicator of someone else's spiritual maturity.

Loving God isn't something you should fake. It is also not something that you can trick someone who *is* Spirit-filled into believing. Anyone who regularly spends time in God's presence will be able to tell if you are faking it. The attractive part of someone who genuinely loves God is the genuine part of it. You can't get right with God to get a girlfriend. You have to get right with God because you want to. You have to be hungry for Him on your own. Finding God through a relationship before you find Him on your own makes the relationship a spiritual crutch, and if you lose that crutch, things in your life will start to come crashing down.

To be spiritually healthy, we need to be actively seeking out God's word and His will. We need to be in a constant state of growth. Becoming more like God can't be passive. It requires action and constant attention. There's not a certain level of faith or good works that you can arrive at and be deemed "spiritually healthy." Being spiritually healthy is a state of seeking God first in everything you do, and every day working toward becoming who He desires you to be. It's becoming more like Jesus.

You know what is interesting about these three areas of your health? While they seem to all be separate—separate areas of life, separate pieces of who you are—they all work together and feed off of one another. When you begin to improve in one area, the others begin to improve as well. As you begin to take care of yourself, you gain self-confidence and begin seeing yourself the way God sees you. As you begin to let go of baggage, it allows God to work in other areas of your life that were overshadowed and obscured by that baggage. As you seek God's desires for you, you begin to see the places where you are holding on to things you shouldn't and you begin to take pride in becoming the best version of yourself. If you start with one, the others will begin to follow.

Like I mentioned before, you can't force these changes. You will either give up, fail, or people will see through the charade. But, if you are truly looking for a man or woman of God to spend your life with, these are things you've got to start to work on, both for yourself, and to be ready for that person when they finally come along.

Lesson 8: Sometimes You *Do* Have to Change for a Relationship

I meant what I said and I said what I meant.

When people tell you that you should never change for a relationship, they're right and they're wrong. You don't need to change how you dress, how (or if) you wear makeup, what body shape you have, what makes you laugh, or what interests you have for a relationship. Those are the things that make you unique. But, there are pieces of us that sometimes do need to change before we get into a relationship.

There are things within us that sometimes keep people away from us. Things like pride, arrogance, and anger can make us unattractive to know, let alone date. The same goes for people who capitalize on or create situations where they can laugh at others' expense. Those are the ugly pieces inside of us. Sometimes they are so small that we don't notice them there, but God sees them. Even the small things have a way of coming out, making themselves known and straining or ruining relationships. These are the things we need to work to change if we want to have successful friendships and relationships.

Some other things you need to change may be when, how, and in whom you place trust, how you judge people, and what your standards are. If you cannot trust anyone, your relationships will be short-lived because trust fuels relationships. If you trust everyone, you may give people who don't deserve it a foothold in your life. If you trust too soon, you may get burned. Mostly, if you trust any human more that you trust God, you are mistaken. No human can keep a promise like God can. If you judge people in one glance, that's got to go too. You know that people can't uncover all of the layers you're made of in one look, so why do you expect that you can do that to other people? If you have the "ability" to determine with one look that someone is not worthy of a date (or even a friendship) with you, you've got some big changing to do.

Perhaps, your "fatal flaw" in relationships is that you need to control things: control your time together, control when and where you go out, control who the other person sees and is friends with. You know what to say, when to say it, and how to say it to get exactly what you want. I'm telling you now: Let. That. Die. That is a symptom of something so much deeper in your heart and you need to spend time talking to Jesus about how He is going to fix that. You will never have a healthy relationship if you need to control the other person that way. A relationship isn't a power struggle. It's a partnership.

"Choose a battle partner not a trophy" —(Andrew Colón).

Humans, especially Christians, have this habit of expecting perfection from anyone they are in a relationship with. It's actually somewhat comical to me that we know how difficult it can be to aim for that life of perfection that Jesus lived, and yet we expect to find someone else who is perfect to have a relationship with. When I talk about changing your standards, I don't mean accepting less than you deserve. What I mean is figuring out the difference between "perfect" and "perfect for you." Perfect is impossible, and when you push people aside because they have small flaws, you miss out on amazing people. (Side note: Isn't it amazing how God offers Himself to us in perfection and yet knows we can't give perfection back?!) But, you can find perfect for you. Perfect for you is someone who loves you and lifts you up in spite of their flaws and yours. Stop holding out for perfection that will never come and start holding out for who God deems as perfect for you.

I'd never tell you to become someone you're not to gain a boyfriend or girlfriend. When things need to change in you and about you, they are the evil, hateful, hurtful, and poisonous parts inside that keep you from becoming more like Christ. They are the parts of our sinful and prideful nature. Those things need to be addressed in all of us, and perhaps for you, those things are getting in the way of the relationship you desire. Or maybe, they are getting in the way of you becoming the person that God desires.

Chapter 12
Worth the Wait

Waiting is quite honestly one of *the* worst things. Especially when the thing you desire is right in front of you and you can't have it. Like at Christmas, when all of the presents are wrapped and under the tree, but you can't look at what they are. I always go shopping with my mom on Black Friday and she often will buy me clothes or shoes that I find in the store that I like, but she makes me wait until I unwrap them on Christmas morning to wear them. That is arguably worse than not knowing what is wrapped and under the tree because I already have expectations and ideas of what I plan to do with these items that are already mine, yet unavailable at the moment. When we desire things, the expectations we build up and the plans we make prematurely are what make the waiting so difficult.

I don't think that waiting is supposed to be easy though. I think that God always uses times of waiting to teach us something. He teaches us about Himself; He teaches us about ourselves. For many people, it is hard to trust God when He asks us to wait, and if someone has been waiting for an extended time, feelings of defeat and wavering may begin to creep their way into the mind. Kristene DiMarco wrote these lyrics in her song "Take Courage":

> *Take courage my heart*
> *Stay steadfast my soul*
> *He's in the waiting*
> *He's in the waiting*

Waiting often seems impossible, like if another day goes by you may burst from the pressure, excitement, stress, or whatever other emotions it is bringing to your life. But, *He* is in the waiting. Whatever season of life you are in, He is there. He stands beside you and waits with you, hoping that you will open your eyes and ears to what He desires to show you as you wait *together*. Waiting is supposed to be difficult. It is supposed to challenge us. It often breaks us down so that we can be built back up again into something new and better.

In times of waiting, I have often found myself biding my time until I get what I want. Simply doing whatever I can to last just another month, just another week, just another day, because surely that is when what I desire will come to me. And when it doesn't come, I again convince myself it will just be a little more time. This is what waiting is like outside of God's protection and without His company. Without Him, our waiting is like walking in circles, and, more times than not, when the walk ends, it leaves us dizzy and with no sense of direction. When we find ourselves in seasons of waiting without God's direction, waiting becomes unbearable. When we wait for something and do not accept or acknowledge the glimpses God gives us of His plan through the waiting, it begins to seem pointless. And if you are waiting for something or someone outside of God's will, it may indeed be pointless.

Another danger when it comes to waiting for things is giving up on something God has promised you or asked you to wait for because you aren't seeing results fast enough. In relationships, this can look like several things. It can be settling for someone who treats you as less than you are. It can be accepting the first person to come along because you feel lucky to have anyone at all. It can be seeking out whoever you can find to settle down with because you're the last of your friends to be single. It can be changing into a version of yourself that people tell you is more desirable. None of those things are what God desires for you, and when you give up waiting, when you settle, you end up in a place you were never meant to be.

I was scrolling through social media one day and came across a post written by a friend from college. Her words were simple, yet profound: "Please don't settle for something you know isn't God's plan for you just because you're tired of waiting" (Samantha Tice).

How often do we settle? How often do we try to take control back from God when His will doesn't work fast enough? I pray that you do not make a habit of settling for less, but if you do, I ask you to consider this: Where would you be if God got tired of waiting for you? Who would you be if God settled for the person you were when you first came to Him because you were "taking too long" to change?

Besides the fact that God continues to wait for us to become the person He desires for us to be, there's also the fact that anything God plans for us is far greater than what we can plan for ourselves. Settling because God's plan isn't coming to completion soon enough is depriving yourself of something grander and more meaningful than you could imagine. When you begin to feel weary in your waiting, whether it is waiting for a spouse or something else you desire, I implore you to remember the message that myself and Samantha have brought to you: when you settle because you are tired of waiting, you are settling for less.

There has to be some upside to waiting for things, right? Right. When we don't give up on the waiting, when we don't settle for what is in front of us right now, we have the opportunity to discover and acquire the things that God has for us. I'll tell you this, it is *hard* to be in that season of waiting. It is difficult to wait for the person God has for you when everyone around you seems to have found them. There have been times in that waiting where I have felt overwhelming loneliness, where I've felt deprived of what I thought I was owed, and where I have felt like giving up or settling, but Christ has been there through all of the waiting. He has been there to lift me up on the days where I feel weary. He is the one that holds my heart together when the enemy would seek to tear it apart. He has been there to remind me that He has something beautiful in store for me if I continue to hold on to His promises.

When I knew it was time to break up with the boy I dated all through my freshman year of college, the idea that I would have to wait for someone else to come along was a frightening one. It was so frightening that I considered being disobedient in what God was telling me so that I would not have to start over or wait any longer. At nineteen years old I was ready to settle for an eventual life of arguments and unhappiness because the mere thought of waiting for someone to come along who was better for me was too much. Thank God that the enemy didn't win that battle in my life. Waiting for God's plan can not only bring you to something better in the end, it can protect you from something harmful in the present. That was 7 years ago and I am still waiting. Is it hard sometimes? Yes, but I know it will be worth it. I chose to wait for the man that God had for me rather than settling for what was in my present grasp, and I was spared an unfulfilling version of my future.

Once again the idea that a young person who comes out of college single is somehow behind in life comes to mind. Nowhere in the Bible does it say that you must marry young to be happy or that you must marry young to be in God's will. I don't know why we act like someone who gets married at twenty-two is any happier than someone who gets married at thirty-two. When you find the right person, there is no measure of the happiness they can bring you. In fact, it is arguable that the person who doesn't find the love of their life until age thirty-two will place a higher value on that relationship when they find it because of the time and effort it took to get there. The longer we wait to receive our deepest desires, the more satisfying they are when they finally come. Don't misunderstand me. I'm not saying that people who get married young don't value their marriages or their spouse, but there is a different type of significance placed on something you have waited and prayed so long for.

In college, I had a professor/mentor/friend who had to wait longer than what most people would consider "normal" to find her husband. Amy's story is one that has both scared and inspired me at times. You see, Amy didn't find her husband until she was in her thirties. The waiting was a long and painstaking process. The enemy tried to come against her and make her question why she was left single for so long. *Am I not pretty enough? Am I not good enough? Do I not deserve this?* That's what the enemy puts into our minds. Sometimes he even uses other people to make us think those things. That's not what God desires for us.

Amy endured the waiting process much longer than I think any of us desire, and the thought of waiting that long to find my husband was not a thought I wished to entertain. But to see Amy and her husband is to see love. Seeing how God has used them, how he has worked in their lives, and how much love they have for each other is incredible. It is something that only could have been God ordained. Amy's story tells me that when it comes to God's plans, timing is never an issue. He is never late, but when His plans come to fruition, they will be well worth the time they took to arrive.

It can be easy to give up on the hope that you have to find a husband or wife. It can be easy to settle for what is in your grasp presently. But,

If it's not in God's plan, it's not worth your time.

DiMarco continues in her song:

Hold onto your hope
As your triumph unfolds
He's never failing
He's never failing

When the right person—God's person—comes along it *will* feel like triumph, and it will feel like triumph because it will be triumph. Triumph over your insecurities. Triumph over your doubts. Triumph over the defeated person that Satan wishes for you to be. So hold on to hope. God never fails to fulfill His promises to us, and His promises are always worth the time and effort it took to get to them.

Chapter 13
Rejection

Rejection is a part of life. Yes, it is one of the less favorable parts of life, but it's one we endure nonetheless. Everyone experiences rejection in some form or another. You didn't make the team. You didn't get the job or the promotion. You didn't get accepted into the college of your dreams. And, perhaps the reason you're reading this, the girl or guy you were after turned you down. No one likes that feeling of rejection.

Being turned down for something or by someone can lead to a flood of emotions. Some of those come from God, a lot of them come from the enemy, and it's not hard to sort out who each feeling comes from. Satan takes rejection as an opportunity to make you feel defeated, shameful, and like a failure. He uses it to whisper lies to you that make you question God's processes and His sovereignty. "Why would you let me feel this pain, God?" "Why didn't you keep me from this rejection and embarrassment?" "Shouldn't you have been able to spare me?" These questions begin to hint at the idea that God doesn't know our pain—that He doesn't see our struggles. Even though we know that is not the truth, those thoughts still seem to creep their way into our minds. John 10:10, ESV says, "The thief comes *only* to steal and kill and destroy…" (italics mine). *That* is Satan's goal: destruction.

But that is not God's goal. That word *but* is a powerful one. When we look in the Bible, that word often leads to our rescue and redemption. That word leads us to the freedom God desires for us to have from all of those things that Satan wills us to be. I'm not talking about the instances where "but" gets used as an argument or excuse.

I'm not talking about those times where it is interjected as an effort to take back control from God. I'm talking about those times when in ourselves we found fear, hopelessness, failure, disappointment, and doubt, but God arrived and turned it around. It is a pause, and a continuation. It is a comma or a breath between the old and destitute and what God desires to see within us.

>...*but God* remembered Noah... (Gen. 8:1, ESV)

>...you meant evil against me, *but God* meant it for good... (Gen. 50:20, ESV)

>...*but God* will ransom my soul... (Ps. 49:15, ESV)

>...my flesh and my heart may fail, *but God* is the strength of my heart... (Ps. 73:26, ESV)

>...*but God* was with him... (Acts 7:9, ESV)

>...*but God* raised Him on the third day... (Acts 10:40, ESV)

...and on and on it goes. A breath; a pause. Satan intended evil, but God intended good. Satan intended weakness, but God intended strength. Satan intended pain, but God intended healing.

Those negative, bitter, defeated, and broken feelings are the ones that Satan tries to distract us with in the midst of rejection. Those moments where we begin to believe that the heartache may be pushing us toward something bigger and better are our "but God" moments. When we don't get what we want, Satan's promptings to wallow in self-pity have a mysterious way of overshadowing other things around us—things like God's reassurance that He is working the situation out in the way that only He can. We need to learn to pay closer attention to those "but God" moments.

While Satan desires that you should spend your time dwelling in darkness, God has grander plans for your life. 1 Peter 2:9, ESV says, "But you are a chosen race, a royal priesthood, a holy nation, a people for his own possession, that you may proclaim the excellencies of him who called you out of darkness into his marvelous light."

God has called you out of the darkness. He has set a calling upon your life. If you are not trusting fully in God when rejection comes, the enemy will have a foothold in your heart and life. And if he gains that foothold, it could allow him to quickly tear down things in your life that you (and God) have spent years building.

When rejection comes, God's goal is to show you and teach you something new. That feeling that says "there must be something (or someone) better," that one is from God. God doesn't close doors without opening new ones. He doesn't wish to trap you in some endless hallway between where you are and where you could be. When one opportunity or relationship ends, there is another one. You just might have to spend a little time looking for it or waiting for it. Sometimes doors close to prevent you from the brokenness you would have experienced if you walked through them. Sometimes they close to build your faith. Sometimes the door that closes is something good, but God wants to offer you something better down the line. Whatever the reason is, it happened out of God's love for us and out of His desire to see us become the best version of ourselves.

Hearing that truth doesn't necessarily make rejection any easier when it comes. Rejection can be really difficult to deal with. The more time, energy, and hope you put into something, the worse it feels when it doesn't happen. There *is* a way to soften the blow of rejection though. Stop putting your faith in yourself. Stop putting your faith in how beautiful or charming or capable *you* are and start putting your faith and trust in how capable God is.

When you invite God on this journey of waiting and hoping from the beginning, He is already there to support you in your sadness/disappointment, and He will have begun preparing you ahead of time to meet that closed door He knows is coming. Making Jesus the center of every relationship, every date, and even every crush is kind of like taking preventative medicine. You have the cure ahead of time, so when illness sets in it doesn't last as long, doesn't affect you as much, and sometimes it doesn't come at all.

.

I've been in a relationship where I sought God at every turn. I made Him a part of every decision I made, and when it came to an end, I was surprised at how quickly I was able to move on. I was so deeply invested in that relationship that I didn't understand how the breakup didn't debilitate me. When I look back though, I can see how He began preparing my heart way before that relationship ended. He saw the end from a long way off and began administering that preventative "medicine"—also known as His love and grace—so that when it arrived, I could get through it with minimal damage.

I've experienced that preventative piece of God's love other times too. It's tough to put emotional stock in a relationship that you know may never happen. It's tough to put your feelings out there when you don't expect the feelings to be mutual. I've been there. The only reason I wasn't in agony afterward is that I had given control over to God from the beginning. He knew about the stress and worry and sadness that would come and He was prepared. He got me through.

That is what it can be like to walk with God through hard things like rejection and heartache. In putting God first, He can take a situation that could have broken your heart, and leave it only slightly bruised. Sad, hurt, disappointed, but not broken.

Something I didn't really understand until recently is how much courage it takes to walk up to someone and tell them how you feel about them with the expectation of being rejected. I mean, telling someone you have feelings for them is difficult in general, but it is way easier when you have evidence that they have feelings back. Doing it with no clue of the outcome? That is hard to do. Those are the situations that I *really* hope you have given God control in, because taking that big a step and having your worst fear come true is something that only God can get you through.

For every confession of feelings (that does not end up being mutual) there are two sides: the one with feelings and the one without. I want to take a minute to talk to the person on the side of the conversation without the feelings. Those talks aren't easy for you either. It can be hard to know how to respond in the moment and how to act around that person after the fact. I understand that dilemma well. There's this thing that happens in you—especially if you're good friends—where you simultaneously don't want to hurt them, but you also don't want to give them the wrong idea. Then, you start to analyze every interaction you've had with them to figure out if you somehow led them on.

Unfortunately, I have to confess that I have reacted poorly in this situation multiple times. In the initial conversation I do fine, but it is in interactions afterward that I have failed to behave the way I should. My tendency is to overcompensate. Where they may have liked spending time with me, I stopped hanging out with them completely and even avoided them in social settings. Where they may have mistaken my being nice for my liking them, I stopped being nice and became pretty mean. In my poor attempts at fixing where I may have given them the wrong idea, I ended up hurting them even worse. I'm not sure if you can relate, but I definitely don't like that version of myself.

In these awkward situations, people tend not to know what to do. Every situation is unique, so I can't give you a script to follow, but speaking as someone who has experienced both perspectives, I can give you an idea of what you may want to try to do in this situation if and when it comes.

If you are going to tell someone you have feelings for them, try to pick neutral ground. You don't want that person to feel like you are trying to manipulate them because you chose some sentimental place or are surrounded by your friends. Keep it simple. You don't need to make an uncomfortable situation worse by dragging it out or oversharing. Tell them you have no expectations and mean it. If they've given you no indication of feelings, you can't expect them to fall for you when you express yours, and you can't get mad at them for that. Most of all, give them space. Don't press them for a response and don't try to force your friendship back to normal. Let them know that if they want to talk about it further, it's their decision. Let them know that when they are ready to start working toward friendship again, it's up to them.

If you have been approached by someone and they begin to express feelings they have for you, don't panic and don't shut down. Be honest and straightforward with them. For all the strength it is taking them to talk to you, they at least deserve your honesty. Listen to them and do not interrupt them. If you know how you feel and have a clear enough head to answer, don't make them wait for your response. If you're not sure how you feel or just need time to process, you're allowed to tell them that you need time to think, but you cannot leave it at that. You have to answer them eventually. You can't be mad at them for having feelings for you since it's not something they can help. When they offer you space, take the time you need and then do everything you can to get back to the friendship you had before. Don't be mean. Don't cut them out. They are the one that was vulnerable, and as hard as the situation may be for you, it's harder for them.

Are we all perfect all the time? No. Will you always act those ways in this type of situation? No, but being prepared ahead of time will help you respond in a better way than you would being caught off guard or if you just try to wing it.

I think it is important to bring you back to where I started in this chapter. Rejection will come in one form or another, *but* it is not an ending. There's that word again. Don't allow Satan to use rejection to pin you down and make you miserable. God wants you to see rejection as the place He can begin to move; as the place He can breathe new life into you once again.

> *In myself I am weak, but in Christ I am strong.*
> *In myself I am broken, but Christ makes me whole.*
> *In myself I have fear, but Christ clothes me in peace.*
> *In myself I find death, but Christ died to give me new life.*
> *In myself rejection would destroy me, but in Christ it makes me something new.*

Chapter 14
What's Next?

So after all that we have talked about, you must be wondering what is next. After all of these lessons and after all of this learning, what do you do? The answer is far simpler than you're hoping for. The answer is that what comes next is up to you and God. I'm not some genie or fortune teller that is promising a magical fix to your love life. The point of this book is to teach you (and the church as a whole) to evaluate the way you look at relationships and being single. God may be calling you to something beyond a relationship right now. He may be asking you to make some sacrifices. I can't give you some five-step solution to your dating woes. All I have to offer you is Christ.

Trust me, *I know* that sounds like your typical Christian response, but it is the truth. The most I can give you is Christ. And, really, He's not mine to give since He has already given Himself to you. The fullness of God in your life and in your relationships hinges on what *you* are willing to surrender and on how obedient you are willing to be. My pastor preached a sermon on obedience recently and he made the point that God isn't sitting around in heaven telling you to do things just because He is bored. He isn't telling you to jump just for the amusement of seeing you jump.

I cannot think of a time where I have been obedient and it has not resulted in greater faith, greater opportunities, greater gifts, greater peace, or greater joy. I *can* think of plenty of times when my disobedience has made me miss out on things. This life isn't about knowing the outcome, seeing every step, or getting your own way. It's about being obedient in everything God asks of you. I can't force you to be obedient. I can't force you to love Christ. I can't force you to accept His help. All I can do is reach out to you where you are—lost, broken, hurting, alone—and remind you that you have a Heavenly Father who loves you and wants what's best for you. He's not looking for submission for the sake of submission. He's looking for obedience so that His blessings can be released upon your life.

If you feel lost or stuck right now, I would encourage you to spend time in prayer seeking out what God wants for you. Honestly, it doesn't matter if you need direction in relationships or in some other area of your life. Prayer is always the first step. God may already know what you're going through, but His desire is that you willingly bring your requests to Him. Seek His will in your life and seek His will in your relationships. Beyond that, you need to find your strength, comfort, love, and direction in Christ so that you don't try to find it in a relationship. Finding worth in anything other than Christ is a recipe for disaster.

I've been blessed in the sense that I have had the opportunity to see what it looks like for people to be in healthy, God-centered relationships and what it looks like for people to be in unhealthy relationships. Sometimes, the only reason I've seen the difference is because God opened my eyes to see it. Hopefully when you look around at the Christian couples that you spend time with, you're seeing good examples. Hopefully you see people like Rachel and Josh, two of my best friends from college who never let their relationship separate them from their friendships, who pray together and discuss what God wants from them individually and as a couple, and who do ministry together. Or, hopefully you see people like Angie and Joel, who intentionally set aside scheduled time for each other every week so that the craziness of work, kids, ministry, and life in general never eclipses their relationship, and who stay faithful to one another and to God even when crisis tries to overcome them. Those are the types of couples that have set examples in my life for what I desire a relationship and a marriage to look like. God placed them there, and if you look hard enough, I would venture a guess that you have some of them in your life as well.

A lot of people get so focused on relationships that they forget to include God. Or, they want them so badly that they try to do it without God's help or without His blessing. This is where we have a screwed up concept of relationships. Being focused on Christ and letting Him lead in that area removes the pressure and the stress. Try that in your life and see what God does with your relationships. See what he does with other things in your life. I think that relationships are often the hardest things to give over to God, but if you can give up control there, I'm positive your whole life will begin to change in the best way possible.

It comes back to tuning in to what God wants to show you and teach you. If you begin to turn down the volume of other people's expectations and turn up the volume of God's, you will see and hear things from Him that you weren't noticing before. I don't claim that as an easy thing to do. Many people have a hard time with this, and that is why the attitude change needs to happen church-wide. As a church, we *have* to stop forcing our own ideas of what other people's lives should look like. We *have* to teach people—especially our impressionable, still developing young people—that there is not one specific "right" way for their lives and relationships to play out. It's not something that is going to be easy to change and it's not going to happen overnight, but it begins with people trying. It begins with *you* trying.

I'll tell you something that anyone who knows me will agree with: I am the *most* awkward, timid, and fearful person when it comes to feelings and relationships. Most of that has to do with my personality. I don't *do* vulnerable, not well anyways. That's why it was comical to me when God said, "Hey, Bethanne, you're going to write a book. Oh, and it's going to be about relationships/why it's okay to be single." I didn't want to be single. I saw singleness as a sort of deficiency. I thought I didn't have enough personal experience with relationships to give anyone advice. It is a topic I was convinced would make me feel too vulnerable.

Now, it's comical to think I ever questioned God in this endeavor. Now, it's silly to think about how my whole body was shaking uncontrollably the first time I read the introduction to someone. You know what else? I'm a different person now. I told you at one point that we're all learning here, and I don't think I realized how true it was when I said it. Every step of the way, in every chapter, God has taught me something. He has shown me His grace and goodness in my life. He has broken my heart for the pain He feels when His children are hurting. Heck, He was teaching me a lot of these things for the first time while I was writing them.

All this time and I'm still no expert though. I still have room to improve. I tell you this to convey the importance of being obedient to everything God asks of you. Yes, even the things you don't feel equipped for. God won't send you into battle alone and unarmed. If I had been disobedient in writing this book because I felt incapable, I would still be broken. I would still be living in defeat over singleness. Worst of all, I would be living outside of God's will, and outside of God's will is a place that I *never* want to be.

This book is my love letter to you, from one single person to another. The idea that there are young people who feel alone and unwanted because they are single is heartbreaking to me. It breaks my heart because I don't want other people to feel that pain that I have felt before. But even more than that, it breaks my heart because I know how life-changing it is when you are able to move past those feelings and see in yourself what God sees when He looks at you. It is my prayer for you that you find the strength and the resolve to stand up for yourself and be proud of what God is doing in your life through your singleness. That's a mindset and a confidence I cannot simply will for you to have. That is something that you are going to have to work hard at every day; but when you reach it, you'll see how incredibly worth it it was. Until then, I'll leave you with one final lesson:

Lesson 9: Be Who God Has Asked You to Be and the Rest Will Come...as *He* wills.

About the Author

Bethanne Milton is a twenty-something, (you guessed it) single girl from southeastern Massachusetts. Singleness, however, is not what defines her, nor is it something that God has ordained for her whole life. She is a teacher, a singer, a writer, an artist, an athlete, a reader, and a child of God. Having been born and raised in Massachusetts, Bethanne is a devoted fan of all New England Sports teams. She herself spent many years playing on baseball, basketball, and field hockey teams. Now she spends much of her free time re-watching 2000s television shows and making crafts.

After graduating from the University of Valley Forge in Phoenixville, Pennsylvania, in 2017, Bethanne returned home to Massachusetts where she became a teacher. Just a short drive from where she grew up, she is blessed to be able to teach everyone's favorite subject—math—to everyone's favorite age group—middle school. Bethanne has always loved math and tries to create activities where her students are able to have fun while learning. Her students' all-time favorite activity was an escape room. In addition to teaching, Bethanne is a volunteer worship leader at the church she attends.

Bethanne is dedicated to living a life that is pleasing to God. She strives to bring honor to God in each and every task she begins. Writing her book, *Single*, was a step in obedience that stretched her more than she could have imagined. While she did "write the book," she does not claim to be any type of expert on singleness or relationships. God is continuing to teach her on a daily basis what these things look like in light of His word, His plan, and His holiness.

CPSIA information can be obtained
at www.ICGtesting.com
Printed in the USA
BVHW030727231121
622259BV00004B/340